5/11

5/11

BETTER THAN BOMBPROOF

BETTER THAN BOMBPROOF

New Ways to Make Your Horse a Solid Citizen and Keep You Safe
On the Ground   In the Arena   On the Trail

Sergeant Rick Pelicano

with Eliza McGraw

TRAFALGAR SQUARE
North Pomfret, Vermont

First published in 2010 by
Trafalgar Square Books
North Pomfret, Vermont 05053

Printed in China

Library of Congress Cataloging-in-Publication Data

Pelicano, Rick.
  Better than bombproof : new ways to make your horse a solid citizen and keep you safe on the ground, in the arena, and on the trail / Rick Pelicano ; with Eliza McGraw.
      p. cm.
  Includes index.
  ISBN 978-1-57076-436-3
  1. Horses–Training. I. McGraw, Eliza R. L. II. Title.
  SF287.P449 2010
  636.1'0835–dc22
                              2010004266

Book design by Carrie Fradkin
Front cover design by RM Didier
Typefaces: Frontpage, ITC Century Condensed, RubinoSansICG

10 9 8 7 6 5 4 3 2 1

DEDICATION

To Anne and Elliott

CONTENTS

PREFACE

Better than Bombproof expands on the information from my first book *Bombproof Your Horse.* I felt a second book was necessary because most of us are not lucky enough to have a 100-percent-bombproof horse—one that never flinches, spooks, spins, or bolts. A solid foundation in basic schooling will give you the tools needed to build confidence and to manage your horse under stress, so in these pages I emphasize the importance of schooling your horse and how it relates to bombproofing.

I show you how schooling exercises improve your ability to negotiate obstacles, multitask in the saddle, and manage your horse. The main equine "model" used in this book is our horse Elliott, an 18-year-old Danish Warmblood, and a very good example of the point I'm trying to make in this book. He was a police horse at one time, but he can still be "hot." This is just his personality. However, his high level of schooling gives his rider the tools to manage him when he gets excited or anxious.

With this in mind, *Better than Bombproof* starts with a review of basic schooling principles—on the ground and in the saddle. Of course you don't have to stay in a traditional riding ring to school your horse properly. This can be done anywhere and anytime. I also discuss how schooling fits into the bombproofing process: There is a chapter on common problems that I frequently run into with my students that can lead to much bigger issues; and a section detailing "compound" bombproofing describes situations where you must multitask in the saddle. These scenarios require you to perform one task while the horse is potentially distracted by another issue altogether. For example, one "compound" lesson I discuss is shooting from horseback. I have been asked how to train horses to deal with this many times over the years, mostly by actors who need the skill for historical reenactments, but it is a useful skill for any horse to learn.

The chapter on trailer loading gives you new ways to deal with less confident horses or problem loaders. As a follow up to the information in my first book, I've included more on parades, as well. There are new formations and tips for planning to ride in bigger parades. In addition, I've offered an introduction to drill teams and how to plan a musical ride. This can be a really fun activity in an arena, and for the parades that allow such performances, you can even use your new drill team skills on the parade route.

An important new chapter covers defensive tactics for trail riders. This is a subject I have been asked about by many folks. For years I taught self-defense to civilians (nonriders) through a program at the police department. So I decided to combine my knowledge and share some ways that horseback riders can avoid or counter an assault. You'll find information on the use of pepper spray; using your horse defensively; maintaining a safe distance from an attacker; escaping an assailant; using personal weapons (such as your hands and feet); along with general guidelines for use of force and your social responsibilities.

I conclude with some notes on bombproof training for kids and a section on games that you might not see in your typical "horseback games" book. The ones I've included are mounted police games that my department finds build confidence and teamwork with the officers and horses.

Sergeant Rick Pelicano
Frederick, Maryland

ACKNOWLEDGMENTS

Many people helped make this book possible and I would like to acknowledge them all.

First, I have to thank my wife, Anne. As the main picture model, she worked hard through many photo shoots (and reshoots). She was a good sport and kept her humor even when our horse, Elliott, slipped one day and fell on her. I owe her many more dinners out at her favorite restaurant.

I thank Jeff Kleinman, who started all this in the first place. Eliza McGraw worked wonders on the manuscript and her photography skills are obvious. I also owe a huge "thank you" to Jeni Werts for her talents behind the lens—her pictures tell visual stories. And thank you to all the models who took time out of their busy days to clean their horses and pose for sometimes difficult pictures.

To all at Trafalgar Square Books, I thank you for your patience and assistance with this project. I greatly appreciate Caroline Robbins, who is undoubtedly the most meticulous person I have ever met. We spent many hours on the phone during the editorial process. Thank you to Rebecca Didier, who was a great help with all of the photos and diagrams, and to Martha Cook for her support and guidance.

Thanks to Zynesia Campbell for her work on the various diagrams, and to Gary Jones for his great cartoon creations. The book just wouldn't be the same without his imaginative artwork.

Lastly, I need to thank all the horses in this book, especially our horse, Elliott, and my police duty horse, Guy. Elliott came to us after retiring from the Metropolitan Washington DC Police Department. He is a 17.2-hand, 18-year-old Danish Warmblood. My wife now uses him for her volunteer patrol duties and dressage, and I use him to give private lessons. Elliott is a perfect example of a horse who can be a little hot at times, but is also very manageable and under control because of his extensive background in dressage.

Guy has been in service for about 15 years now. He is an Oldenburg with a hunter/jumper background. We were the 2006 North American Police Equestrian Championship Equitation Champions. Now that he is a veteran, he has developed a knack for falling asleep any chance he gets while we are on patrol. He even falls asleep during parades if we are standing around long enough. Check out the Nerf ball toss pictures on p. 161. He really could care less. What a Guy!

1

Review—
What It Means to Be
"Bombproof"

Introduction

I am Sergeant Rick Pelicano of the Maryland National Park Police. I have been with the department for over 20 years and have spent most of that time in charge of training horses and officers. I am also the author of *Bombproof Your Horse: Teach Your Horse to Be Confident, Obedient, and Safe No Matter What You Encounter.*

Before we begin to explore new "bombproofing" territory, including complex scenarios you and your horse might confront in your day-to-day riding life, it is important that we go over some of that which I discussed in my first book. This chapter reviews the basic bombproofing concepts and definitions of the terms that are the foundation of the exercises and instructions in *Bombproof Your Horse.* All these concepts apply to ground training as well as work under saddle.

Before we begin, remember: Your riding skill and your horse's level of schooling are both equally important to your success. Do not "overhorse" yourself; if your horse is green and unreliable and you are still learning, you should spend more time on the true basics of riding and horsemanship before you undertake a bombproofing program.

Key Concepts

Here are some important words and phrases I use, which will help you understand the training techniques in this book.

Bombproof
Horse people use the word "bombproof" to describe a horse that is confident, safe, and

unlikely to spook. It stems from the idea that if you were to detonate a bomb near the horse, he would be so quiet and sane that he wouldn't startle, even at something so extraordinary. (Obviously, I don't advise trying anything so radical. The term is extreme to make a point.) Synonyms for bombproofing include to *habituate* and to *desensitize,* and all three condition a horse to be comfortable with a long list of distractions and potentially scary situations. This methodical system of exposure turns any horse into a more pleasurable, confident, and safer mount.

Comfort Zone

This is the place at which a horse is comfortable dealing with a threatening stimulus. He's still aware of the stimulus, and may even be concerned about it, possibly taking a step back or tilting his head as he walks by. But, he's not so worried that his flight response kicks in: You should still be able to exert influence on him with your aids. In any given situation, the horse's comfort zone can be related to distance, physical appearance, or the intensity of a stimulus, which can be anything from a backfiring car to a child holding a balloon. Many horses find spooky objects even in the most ordinary things, from a blowing plastic bag to a jump that moved to a different place in a familiar riding arena.

To help a horse *increase* his comfort zone you need to find the boundary, or edge of it, and push him to stretch a bit beyond it. You need to "tread the line" and find the right balance just beyond the place where he remains relaxed but before the place where he is totally uncomfortable. You need to "breach" the boundary in order to teach him to accept a new stimulus, which in turn takes him to the next level of training. (See *Bombproof Your Horse* for a thorough explanation of the comfort zone.)

You can place an obstacle on the ground for him to walk over—a tarp, for example. You may

first need to *decrease* the stimulus by folding the tarp to a width of 1 foot, thus making the obstacle much smaller. Nearly every horse can easily step over something so little. And, with loud noises such as gunfire, the horse's existing comfort zone may be as much as a tenth of a mile away from the sound, or he may be okay at 100 yards. There is no step too small, since any move closer to the noise positively influences his training and increases that crucial comfort zone. To manipulate the intensity of the gunfire experience and avoid the distance factor, you can start by reducing his exposure to loud noise by using a cap gun. Next, you can switch to a starter pistol, and ultimately to a standard firearm using a blank. (In bombproofing clinics, where I train horses to tolerate gunfire, we never use live rounds, by the way—blanks only.) I discuss accustoming horses to gunfire in this book on p. 85.

How do you decide how much to ask of your horse when in the process of desensitizing? Well, you have most likely had to manage a situation in which your shying or shaking horse showed you that you had breached the boundary of his comfort zone. When this happens, consider requesting an action that will have a *probable positive outcome*—that is, give the horse a familiar task that he will likely complete successfully and without stress**.** This builds his confidence and chances are—upon completing said task—he will trust you and be willing to go a little beyond his comfort zone and confront a new experience. You must then turn this *new* move into a *familiar* one through *repetition,* which is the glue that makes the lesson stick. It convinces the horse that whatever you are asking him to do isn't harmful or scary. And his assurance will grow with each progressive accomplishment.

Let's use the example of passing a fallen tree along the trail. Perhaps your horse takes an exception to the tree, and turns into a quaking mountain of fear. Rather than immediately confronting the frightening object, turn his attention to something he can do easily, such as a little bit of leg-yielding or trotting a circle. The familiar task will comfort him, build his confidence, and prepare him to face the fallen tree with less inclination to turn and flee. Once you pass the tree, the key, of course, is to pass it again, and again, to make sure your horse has learned the lesson for good.

Progressive Training

As an extension of the comfort zone, once you have acclimatized a horse to the stimulus at a lower level, you must incrementally raise the intensity. This process, which focuses on progression, is called *progressive training*. For example, the 1-foot-wide tarp I mentioned on p. 2 can become 2 to 3 feet wide, then 10, and so on. Progressive training lets the horse build confidence gradually, while giving the rider the least amount of resistance. When the stimulus increase remains small enough, the horse will hardly even notice how far he is pushing himself (fig. 1.1).

Repetition is very important in this process. When the horse exhibits a "flight response," he will require 20 to 30 repetitions to become comfortable with any given stimulus, but should he display only slight apprehension, you can get away with far fewer repetitions. A horse that merely pauses to look at a baby stroller, for example, only needs to walk by it four or five times before he seems to forget it is even there. But, a horse that bolts at the sight of a garbage truck may require far more patience and repetitive training.

The Four "Ts" of Success: Training, Testing, Technique, and Timing

1 Training

This is the process of improving skills—yours or your horse's—through graduated steps. In fact,

1.1 Anne and Elliott negotiate a rubber mat along the rail in the outdoor arena.

training is like climbing a staircase. When you move one step at a time you can reach a very high level, but if you try to skip steps, you never achieve your goal.

When you ride, your aids—hands, legs, and seat—convey to your horse what you want him to do. This is *learned* behavior since it is not natural for a horse to move away from leg pressure or drop his head when he feels you adjust the reins. His instincts may, in fact, tell him to do the opposite. For example, an unschooled horse actually moves *toward* leg pressure because his instinct tells him to deal with a pest by pressing into a convenient object, such as a tree. The horse has to *learn* that your aid is a means of asking a question, not just a torture device. For your horse to do what you ask, he must understand the requests you make.

Moving forward willingly from the leg is the most basic principle your horse needs to understand since it is the foundation for all your other work. When you give him a squeeze with your calves, he should respond reasonably, not act irritated or worse, back up or even buck. When your horse comprehends that a squeeze with

A DAY AT A BOMBPROOFING CLINIC

1.2 A–K In my bombproofing clinics, horses are asked to venture out of their comfort zone and confront new, often "scary" experiences. Through progressive training, we gradually teach participants to negotiate past flares, over tarps, through refuse, around balloons, between flags, and under moveable structures.

both legs means that he should go forward, you can test if he knows what pressure with one leg means—that is, *move sideways.*

Bit acceptance represents another important part of your horse's knowledge. He should be able to relax his jaw and poll to give you that wonderful feeling of "holding hands" with his mouth. An uneducated animal will raise his neck in order to protect his mouth whenever he feels contact with the bit, while a horse that yields to the bit correctly has the trademark arched neck, relaxed back, and swinging hindquarters of a well-trained mount.

During your training time specified for bombproofing, you can do anything you want. You can stay mounted or dismount. You can move obstacles around. You can ask for help from others. You can end on a high note after a moment of success, no matter how small, and decide to call it a day and save bombproofing for another time.

There is much more about training in chapter 3, p. 37.

2 Testing

Self-testing is an important part of training. You should push your horse's comfort zone regularly to note progress and determine if he has advanced to a new level. Self-testing must be done progressively and systematically, just like training; your horse should only be asked to attempt tasks where you can reasonably expect success. If it becomes obvious that you have asked too much of him—for example, if a seasoned jumper bangs his legs or shies at an oxer—make the lesson easier. Lower the jump, or make it into a vertical.

When you are *real-life testing*, however, you have far less control over the situation. You have to find a way through a situation that will not endanger either you or your horse, and the best way to accomplish this is through solid background training. When you're on the trail, for example, and come upon a highly charged situation—such as a crowd of loud dirt bikes— you are testing your horse. In a competition circumstance, such as riding a cross-country course or a dressage test, you are testing your horse. Think of it this way: when you don't have the ability to alter the environment, you are testing, not training. Remember, you can turn any test into a training opportunity.

In any situation, if you need to, dismount and work your horse from the ground (fig. 1.3). In my clinics, I often hear people say that they don't want to get off because they feel the horse is "getting away with something." Some people also feel that getting off is cheating, or that it somehow makes them less of a rider. That is ridiculous! Dismounting is simply part of progressive training. Sometimes you need to take it down a notch to gain the horse's trust and this can mean getting off and working from the ground before climbing back in the saddle to try again when you are both comfortable. You can't achieve much when you are grabbing the reins, fearful for your own safety.

You need *testing* to push your horse to reach new levels, but be patient. Don't attempt more than you and your horse can reasonably handle.

3 Technique

This is how you execute an action or a series of actions. To use a martial arts analogy, think of a fighter throwing a punch. Is that punch delivered accurately, powerfully, and efficiently? Or, is it delivered weakly, ineffectively, and off target? The same questions apply to leg aids and rein contact. These need to be delivered properly to have the desired effect of controlling the horse and keeping both of you safe and comfortable.

Very often, I see a rider "assume the fetal position" when approaching an obstacle her horse might find threatening. The rider assumes this defensive position because she is anticipating a struggle. Instead, she should sit deep in the saddle and maintain leg contact. That way, she is prepared should the horse spook, but at the same time she conveys confidence, which may make her horse less likely to run out on her in the first place—her confidence becomes his confidence.

Even more prevalent than the rider in a fetal position is the ground handler who uses poor technique. The horse pays zero attention to his handler and walks all over her. Just because you are not actually riding your horse does not make him any safer—especially if he's behaving poorly. The section on longeing and ground techniques on p. 11 can help fix groundwork difficulties, which in turn will make any horse a better riding companion.

1.3   Sometimes it makes the most sense to confront a "scary" experience from the ground. Here I work a clinic participant's horse with a longe line before she attempts the obstacle in the saddle.

4 Timing

This is your ability to use the right skills at the right moment. If your horse spins to the left when he sees something that scares him and you never correct him, you have a severe timing issue. The flight response takes over and even if you stay on, your horse is no better trained than he was the first time he executed his spin. On the other hand, if you feel the horse attempting to spin left and you take action *before* he actually does it, you have exhibited good timing. Now, he will remember your correction before he considers spinning on you again.

When the rider fails to act, you become nothing more than a passenger. Good timing encourages good behavior and instills confidence in the horse. If your timing is good, the horse will come to realize that he can depend upon you to keep him safe. That, in turn, will make him less likely to spook or bolt.

Punishment and Reward

When I talk about *punishment*, I do not mean you should *ever* beat a horse. But, if he is acting unacceptably, there needs to be an uncomfortable consequence. When your horse refuses to walk through a shallow puddle, your "punishment" technique may be as simple as using more leg pressure, followed if needed, by appropriate application of your spurs or whip as reinforcement. He just has to know there is an unpleasant result to his disobedience. When leading him on the ground and he walks on top of you, he needs an elbow in his side or a bump on his nose with a chain to remind him to respect your space. Remember that your horse is no toddler: He is a powerful animal who must learn to understand that his disobedience has disagreeable results.

When your horse does proceed as you wish, give him a big pat and a kind word. When you reward him for a positive response, he will become more eager to please you and do your bidding in the future.

1.4 A & B When a horse is frightened of an object, such as this smoking flare, it helps to have other, more seasoned horses negotiating the obstacle at the same time. The unsure horses are usually willing to follow the experienced horses' lead—for example, if they circle close to the flare, the unsure horses will do so, as well.

Active Riding

An active rider is able to manage the horse's flight response—she rides both *proactively* and *reactively*. Controlling impulsion is one of the most important parts of proactive riding: A horse needs to plant his feet in order to make an adverse maneuver, so if you keep his feet moving—in a controlled fashion—you become the one managing the situation. Keeping the horse moving forward is not as difficult or complex as you might think since this kind of active riding does not necessarily mean he has to

move in a straight line. In fact, circling is often the best method to gain the horse's attention and regain influence. As long as you are the one deciding *where* the horse goes forward, you are riding actively and improving the situation.

The active rider also helps herself by noticing when a situation requires more input and when she needs to change what she is doing. Some examples of active riding are:

- Using shoulder-in to ride by or over an obstacle
- Putting a horse on the bit, and using it as a relaxation tool
- Increasing impulsion (such as trotting past an obstacle that the horse is walking by with trepidation or is jigging by nervously)
- Changing the approach to an obstacle (i.e. circling rather than riding directly up to it)
- Dismounting when necessary
- Evaluating a potentially difficult "situation" early enough in order to prevent it from happening

Knowing when to ride with others is another part of active riding. Mounted police and cavalry units like to train in a group setting because of the power of the herd instinct as a training tool. We always train a new police horse alongside a veteran. This helps instill confidence much more quickly than sending him on patrol alone. In my clinics, there is always a good mix: I keep enough reasonably confident horses to assist the less-confident ones. This way, for example, when I see a "traffic jam" of riders trying to cross a tarp because horses are shying and refusing to move forward, I can ask someone with a more experienced mount to lead everyone else across. The scared horses take comfort in another's ability to confront the "spooky" experience, and find out how simple it is to walk across on their own (figs. 1.4 A & B).

Key Bombproofing Strategies

Diversion

Often, *diverting your horse's attention* with a different activity is enough to handle a tough circumstance. In a threatening environment, such as a parade, horse show, or even an unfamiliar trail, any horse can become frightened. In this type of situation, I immediately ask my horse to perform a task, so that he becomes more concerned about my request than his surroundings. For example, I work him at the trot in a circle or figure eight, asking him to bend in the direction he's going. It doesn't matter what you ask as long as you vary your requests, so that your horse is forced to listen. Getting the horse to pay attention to *you*—instead of whatever chaos is around him—is the key factor.

Movement

Letting your horse move is more effective than asking him to stand still. Movement gives him an outlet for his nervous energy and also requires that he *go forward*, which helps prevent evasion.

Reassurance

Sometimes your horse needs you to tell him that everything will be all right. *Letting him look* is always helpful; often, a horse can assess something as non-threatening once he sees what it is. If you are acquainted with horses, you have probably experienced the unpredictable "spook." Because equines have such strong "prey-animal" instincts, even the best-trained among them may shy at something new. Since you can't prevent the occasional spook from happening, you have to ride through it.

First, regain control. If your horse is running away, halt him, and if he wheels around, turn him in the opposite direction. Do something besides freezing in fright. Once you have cor-

1.5 A & B Anne and Elliott suited up for groundwork and appropriately outfitted for bombproofing under saddle.

rected him, move on with your ride. *Ignore the "monster."* Your horse needs to think that you are not frightened—even if you are—so keep as cool as possible to reassure him.

Direction

There are times when your horse cannot muster the courage to walk directly up to a threatening object. In these cases, change your *direction.* Spiral around the item, or approach it from a different angle. Edge closer and closer—remember, you are in charge—even when it pushes the horse, little by little, out of his *comfort zone* (see p. 2). Before he knows it, your mount will be confronting his "monster" head on. Then he can *sniff, touch,* and *evaluate* the bicycle, bush, or other object that is disturbing him, and next time, he will walk by it calmly.

Now that I've discussed the key terms and strategies involved in *basic* bombproofing, get ready for slightly more advanced work!

2

Longeing and Long-Lining

Introduction

There are entire books dedicated to longeing and long-lining the horse. They are important techniques that help horses succeed in all riding disciplines. I only touched on these training methods and their bombproofing benefits briefly in *Bombproof Your Horse,* so here I will go into much more depth.

This chapter discusses different types of longeing and long-lining, as well as the use of a round pen. You probably won't find it necessary to do all of these things in your bombproofing program, but it will help you to understand these training skills, nevertheless, so you can make the most of your time.

What does all this groundwork have to do with bombproofing? I know—you want to get to the good stuff, right? But, if your horse is manageable both from the ground and under saddle, you

will be more successful when you decide to start desensitizing him to new stimuli. And that makes him more predictable and enjoyable to ride.

Look at it this way: The first thing I am concerned with when looking at a new police horse prospect is how well the horse goes under saddle. It is the foundation for any kind of police training or bombproofing. If the horse struggles when he is ridden in an arena, he will be ten times worse under the stress of police training. And, how a horse behaves under saddle is directly related to how he behaves when handled and worked from the ground.

I will talk about longeing first, and then turn to long-lining.

Longeing

So, why not help set the stage for bombproofing

success with a good foundation of groundwork? Longeing is an important part of this basic building block. It is used for many reasons and has many applications for further training. When done properly and regularly, longeing can:

- Teach obedience and discipline
- Correct bad habits
- Exercise or rehabilitate a horse
- Make ground-driving and long-lining easier
- Improve the horse's gaits, rhythm, impulsion, straightness, and flexibility

Before I decide if I need to longe a new horse prior to beginning mounted police work, I assess him to determine his particular needs. A horse that has been competing in dressage or eventing, for example, may not need any longeing at all. Horses that have competed in one of these demanding sports are most likely already proficient at longeing-friendly tasks, such as small-circle work and gait transitions. On the other hand, when a horse has difficulty picking up the right or left canter lead, longeing (or long-lining, see p. 26) may be beneficial to him. It's also a good way to exercise a horse coming off an injury, since longeing or long-lining with a bridle and bit directly transfers ground training to work under saddle. (For a detailed discussion, see p. 37.)

Bear in mind that longeing can be hard on some horses. It may not look stressful, but traveling around a small circle—especially at a canter—can exact a real toll on a horse's legs and joints. Ask your veterinarian to advise you on your horse's soundness before beginning a routine. With young horses in particular, you should be careful not to overdo it. Their bones and joints are more susceptible to stress than those of older horses. Keep sessions short, and closely follow the guidelines your veterinarian sets out for you.

GROUNDWORK SAFETY TIPS

When working your horse from the ground, keep yourself safely outfitted. Wear gloves and barn-safe footwear, such as riding or work boots. Just because you are not riding doesn't mean you can wear flip-flops to work your horse. Take off your spurs so they don't get caught in the lines, and run up the stirrups when working the horse in full tack so they don't bang the horse's sides.

Longeing Equipment

For this sort of work you need a longe line; a longeing cavesson, a halter, or a bridle with a snaffle bit; and a whip—all of which I'll discuss in detail. Before beginning you must note that when you longe in the bridle, you need to make some allowances for the bit. For example, you cannot "snap" the longe line to get the horse's attention as you can when using a cavesson, because this action would catch the horse in the mouth. You also lose the ability to change direction easily. So make an assessment: Does your horse have the temperament to start right away in the bridle, or should you begin your longe work with a cavesson or halter?

Longe Line

When beginning to teach a horse to longe, do yourself a favor and use the shortest line that you can find—even a lead line will do. Most longe lines are about 30 feet (approximately 10 meters) long. I advise using a line 10 to 12 feet in length. The part of the longeing process that requires the most coordination is dealing with excess longe line, so keep it neatly contained in one hand as you longe with the other to prevent you or the horse tripping over it. Avoid longe lines made with a chain at one end. These are unwieldy and the chain can hurt the horse's sensitive muzzle if things get out of hand at any point.

Cavesson

Longeing in a cavesson is best. A cavesson is a headstall with a padded noseband featuring metal rings to attach the longe line (fig. 2.1). The cavesson's noseband should rest on the horse's nasal bone—a little higher than an ordinary noseband—and the throat strap needs to be a little snugger than a regular throatlatch. A quality longeing cavesson is a worthwhile investment if you plan to longe your horse with any frequency. It keeps the horse secure and responsive without your having to worry you will hurt the horse's mouth, which is the case when longeing the horse in a bridle. In addition, when you use a cavesson (or halter) you can teach the horse to change direction without additional effort (see p. 20). When you longe with a bridle and bit (see below), you have to stop and reattach the longe line to the opposite side every time you reverse direction.

Halter

You can use a halter for longeing your horse when you don't have access to a cavesson, or if you simply want to see how your horse goes on the longe line before investing in new equipment (fig. 2.2). Although the cavesson is the more effective choice, if you are concerned only with basic obedience and not poll flexion, a halter can suffice. It should be sturdy and adjusted appropriately.

Bridle

When longeing the horse in a bridle, use a snaffle bit. (Note: I do not recommend that beginners start longeing this way—they should stick

2.1 A correctly adjusted longeing cavesson, with the line attached to the center ring on the noseband.

2.2 You can longe your horse in a halter if you don't have a cavesson. The halter should be sturdy and adjusted properly. Attach the line (without a chain) to the ring under the horse's chin, as shown here.

to a cavesson or halter.) A curb bit should never be used as it could catch the horse's mouth in a painful way, and he would soon understandably reject his longeing lessons.

When using a bridle and bit, you may add side reins. These are very helpful for teaching the horse to flex at his poll and stretch down to the bit. The side reins are attached from the bit to either a surcingle or a saddle. However, there are many considerations here and caution must be used as misapplication of side reins can be detrimental to your horse's physical and mental well-being. (See further discussion on this subject on p. 14.)

Longeing with a bridle and snaffle bit offers advantages not found with the cavesson, such as the horse learns to respond to rein pressure, just as you ask him to do when you are riding him, and the added control improves the horse's way of going.

There are different ways to attach the longe line to the bit. The method is a matter of preference, and the variations offer different types of benefits and drawbacks. The key points to keep in mind are: a) you don't want to hurt the horse's mouth, and b) you need to keep him balanced and forward as he works.

Attaching the Longe Line

The simplest way to work a bitted horse on the longe is to attach the line directly to the snaffle bit. Some people prefer to run it through a bit ring, over the poll and down to the opposite bit ring where it is clipped, which evens out the pressure on each side of the bit and gives you a little extra pressure on the poll. Some feel that gives them extra control, but I think the difference is negligible. Another method is to run the line through the inside bit ring (closest to the inside of your longe circle) and back to the surcingle or saddle where you clip it to an available D-ring or billet (figs. 2.3 A–E). This method helps influence the horse's bend in special cases. Or, you can run the line through the bit ring nearest you and under the horse's chin to the opposite ring. Use the method with which you are most comfortable.

Using Side Reins

To further the riding analogy as you work your horse on the longe, consider adding side reins. They are good for teaching the horse to flex at his poll, and reach for and stretch down to the bit. The side reins are attached from the bit to either a surcingle or saddle (fig. 2.4). I prefer using the saddle, though when you do, make sure the stirrups are out of the way by running them up or crossing them over the saddle.

When attaching side reins for the first time, you must act with caution so the horse does not panic. Buckle both side reins around the saddle's billets first, and then clip the inside rein to a bit ring. Fasten the outside side rein if the horse is comfortable with the inside rein. (Note: When you are longeing the horse, the "inside" is closest to the middle of the longe circle. When you start schooling, the meaning of *inside* and *outside* is a bit more specific: "inside" then refers to the side the horse is bent or flexed toward. See the sidebar on p. 44 for more on this subject.) The side reins should be adjusted snug enough to keep the horse from going "high and hollow," while loose enough to encourage him to stretch down. They should *never* be used to hold the horse's head in an artificial position, but they also should not be so loose they annoy the horse by flapping around.

Whip

You also need some kind of a whip. I advocate using a short longe whip—standard longe whips range from 4 to 6 feet plus a lash of 6 feet or more, but they make "mini" versions for travel, of 3 to 4 feet with shorter lashes. Even better, I find, is a "Handy Stick," a truncated longe whip made popular by horse trainer Clinton Anderson, and available from his Web site (www.downunderhorsemanship.com). The Handy Stick works well because it is short, maneuverable, and the horse can easily see it—particularly if you use a white one.

Longe with a Purpose

Any time you longe your horse you should have a clear purpose in mind, since simply letting him run around in endless circles will not teach him anything. Use each session to accomplish something new or to reinforce basics. This foundation will teach the horse obedience, discipline, respect, and responsiveness.

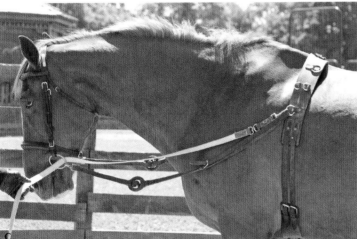

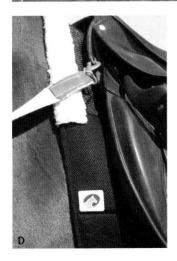

2.3 A–E   There are many ways to correctly attach a longe line when using a bridle and bit. The easiest is to simply attach the line directly to the snaffle ring on the side closest to the inside of your longe circle (A). You can also run the snap end of the line through the inside bit ring, up along the cheek piece, over the horse's poll, down along the outside cheek piece, and snap it to the outside bit ring (B). The many alternatives include running the line through the inside bit ring and clipping it to a billet or D-ring on the surcingle or saddle (C–E).

2.4   Side reins correctly adjusted and attached to a surcingle.

Longeing with a purpose is necessary for green and unruly horses. Many people attend my clinics only to find that their horse pays no attention to them, either on the ground or under saddle. Perhaps he is distracted by the new environment or looking for his stable buddy and totally oblivious to his rider. He displays his distraction and disrespect by "walking all over" his handler on the ground and can be quite dangerous when mounted (see p. 65 for more on inattention in a clinic environment).

In these cases, I often take the horse from the owner and work with him myself—one on one. I use a variety of strategies to calm the horse and reach a mutual understanding so the horse acknowledges my presence and begins to cooperate. While I can do this and thus "save" the rider's clinic experience, it's not a long-term solution. I usually recommend that the rider perform longe work on her own at home so she can get the horse's attention, improve their relationship, and therefore better her riding experience.

Round Pens

The round pen is not a major part of my training program. Although round pens can be used to habituate your horse to some types of obstacles, I generally find them too limiting for bombproofing work. However, for longe work, I love to use a round pen, especially for schooling green horses. We trainers like them because they are actually an artificial aid of a sort. An artificial aid is any item used for communication—crops and spurs are the most common examples—but even something as fundamental as a bit can be viewed as an artificial aid. The round pen can be as helpful as these common riding tools—almost like having a second person helping you with your horse.

If you have ever attempted to longe a green horse out in the open, it is most likely your horse

did not make a nice round circle, but rather repeatedly attempted to run out. He may not have understood what you were asking and instead obeyed his flight instinct out of insecurity. Here is where the round pen comes in handy: The horse cannot run to the outside because there is a wall there. Because of its shape, the pen reinforces what you want the horse to do. Walls and circles are a trainer's best friends.

Making a Round Pen Out of an Arena
If you do not have a round pen, you can use the fence line or wall of your arena to provide the same kind of support. When your arena has rounded corners, longe in a corner area to give your horse a "secure space," much like what you find in a round pen.

When your arena, like most, has square corners, you may face the common issue of your horse evading work by "ducking" into the corner. If this happens, try "rounding" out the corners with some cavaletti or elevated ground poles (fig. 2.5). This isn't as good or convenient as a round pen, but will do in a pinch. The key is to have the horse's surroundings mimic a circle.

Longeing Aids

Whip Position
The whip is a key tool when longeing (and when long-lining—see p. 26). It guides the horse when necessary and motivates him to speed up. You carry the whip in the hand closest to the horse's hindquarters—when longeing left, it should be in your right hand, and vice versa. Remember that every time you change direction, you must switch your whip hand, as well.

You can hold the whip in one of two ways. Many people who longe carry their whips with the "business end" pointed out and away to the side, but I carry mine down along my leg, as I would if I were riding. The whip is oriented

2.5   You can create your own "round pen" by rounding out the corners of your arena with ground poles or cavalletti. This can help you train an inexperienced horse to remain on the longe circle.

with the handle toward my thumb and the end with the lash going out on the pinky side of my hand—that is, in a "backward" position. Most of the time, the whip is behind me, out of the horse's line of vision. I flick my wrist around when I need to, and the whip follows (figs. 2.6 A–C). This way it remains out of the way until I need it, which helps to minimize accidents from inadvertent signals to the horse.

Voice Commands

You use your voice in conjunction with your longe line and whip, and eventually, the horse begins to respond more to your voice and less to any other input. As you work with them, horses respond more to the inflection in your voice than they do to the word itself. They recognize that a louder, higher tone means to go faster, and a more soothing, descending tone means that they should transition downward. Voice commands are a key part of longeing and can supplement rider communication as well.

    "Clicking" your tongue encourages the horse to go more *forward*. Similarly saying something like, "Hup, hup" also tells a horse to *step up his pace*. To *slow down*, use "Whoooooooa," draw-

2.6 A–C   Here you can see how I prefer to hold the longe whip, "backward," with the handle up (A). This position prevents inadvertent whip action as the "business end" is out of the way, but can be employed with a backhand flick of the wrist. Elliott is moving nicely but needs some extra encouragement from the whip, which I provide with a simple move with my right hand (B & C).

ing out the "oh" sound in a soft, relaxed voice. To *halt*, say "Whoa," or "Halt." With "Walk," emphasis the "k" with a business-like staccato. Say "Trot" as "Terrroott," keeping in mind that an upward transition should sound firm and crisp. When asking for "Canter," emphasize each syllable with a higher pitch, while the downward transition back to a slower gait should sound quieter and more relaxed.

I like to use "Halt" to ask a horse to stop, "Easy" to calm, slow, or transition down, and "Quit!" when he does something undesirable. But, you can use whichever phrases you like or those your horse already knows. Just be consistent with your command phrases so you don't confuse him. People who talk their horse's head off think their horse understands everything they are saying, but he doesn't. Sure, he recognizes a few words, but he primarily understands the tone you use when you say them.

Body Language

You "speak" with your body as well as your voice when you longe your horse. Stepping toward the horse's front end signals him to slow down or stop, while a step toward his rear end asks him to speed up.

Basic Longe Commands

Walk and Halt

Now you are ready to begin longeing. For the purposes of these directions, I'm going to assume you are using a longeing cavesson (see p. 13).

Begin by standing on the horse's near (left) side next to his head, holding the longe line in your left hand and your whip in your right. You should be facing the horse, slightly toward his rear end. Collect the excess line in an orderly fashion in your right hand, alongside the whip. You need to be very close to the horse at this stage, with maybe only 2 to 3 feet of longe line between you. If you try to enforce this first lesson from further away, say 10 feet, the horse either will ignore your commands entirely or run out on the exercise.

Use the longe line to direct your horse as follows: *Horizontal vibrations* drive the horse away from the center of the circle (where you are). *Upward movement* asks the horse to slow or halt when your voice command alone does not work. Should neither your voice nor your line cue do the job of slowing or stopping the horse, you can give the line a sharp tug, but *only* when you are longeing the horse in a cavesson or halter, and never when using a bridle and bit.

Ask the horse to walk forward by saying "Walk" (see p. 17) and with a circular flick or shake of the whip behind him. (For more on using the whip, see p. 16). You need not touch the horse with the whip—in fact, to start, it is best to keep it away from him whenever you can. Use as little whip motion as you need to encourage movement. If the horse fails to respond, flick the whip again, quickly but gently, just below the horse's hocks. After the horse walks several steps, raise your left hand and say, "Halt," or "Whoa" (figs. 2.7 A & B).

Once your horse begins to understand the drill, you can move away from him, backing away a few steps at a time with each revolution around you. If you started with 2 or 3 feet of longe line, let it out to 4 or 5 feet and attempt the same exercise. If he doesn't get it from your new position, return to the original distance and reconfirm that he understands by repeating the exercise until he obediently halts when asked.

As you move away from your horse, you will gradually adapt a more traditional longeing position, with yourself as the point of a triangle formed by the longe line and whip (see sidebar, p. 22). I like to start with a small circle—let's say 10 or so feet in diameter. Then I increase the size of the circle to 20 feet, so I move from 5 feet away from the horse to 10, and I find that once you are about 10 feet away, you can quickly progress to 15 or 20 feet. However, your

2.7 A & B   In order to teach Elliott to halt on command, I begin close beside him, facing slightly toward his hindquarters. I ask him to walk forward a few steps with a vocal command and flick of the whip (A), and then tell him "Whoa," and raise my left hand to put slight pressure on the cavesson (B).

HALTING ON COMMAND : THE "TURN AND FACE YOU" QUESTION

I know there are many trainers doing work similar to mine, and I in no way mean to disparage anyone with the following comments: Many trainers teach the horse to turn and face them when he comes to a halt on the longe line. I, however, only want the horse to turn and face me when I call him into the circle—that is, when I ask him to do so.

Why do I make this a rule? Because turning to face me means we are on a break. When I call the horse into the center he gets to relax, and I give him a nice pat for a job well done. Otherwise, it is "work time." Also, if you plan to long-line the horse at some point (which I discuss on p. 26), allowing him to turn and face you at the halt could cause him to get tangled in the long lines. So it is a bad habit to encourage at this earlier stage of training.

influence over your horse's movements fades as you enlarge your circle, so always start small.

Remain centered on the horse as he moves. When you ask for him to slow down or halt, orient your body more to his front. Also, raise your hand in conjunction with altering your body position, just as you did when you began the exercise with the halt up close. Eventually the horse will become so tuned in

to your body movements that you will be able to eliminate the hand motion. Early in training, however, continue to raise your hand, and after the horse halts, keep your hand up until you give the verbal "Walk" cue. Then, drop your left hand and use a little whip (only as much as necessary). The horse may walk on simply by seeing your hand motion. When you want the horse to move forward with more impulsion, take a step toward his rear. Repeat this exercise in both directions (fig. 2.8).

2.8 I ask Elliott to step forward with more energy by taking a step toward his hind end and giving the whip a little flip. Notice his inside hind leg stepping well under him and his ear cocked toward me—he's listening attentively to my cues.

2.9 As I longe Elliott to the left, you can see that I am moving in a small circle of my own, inside the larger longe circle—I am not stationary, but moving to accommodate his forward motion and keep the line tension appropriate for the lesson.

Trot

Once the horse is obedient with halt and walk commands, you can move on. Ask for the trot in the same way you did the walk—a bit of whip action, a step toward the rear—but you will, of course, say, "Trot," or "Terrottt" (see p. 17). Begin on a smaller circle and work your way up to a larger one. The drill is basically the same as working on your walk-halt transitions—you are now just training the horse to respond to a new vocal cue and to move in a controlled manner at a higher speed.

Some people think they have to stand rigidly in the center of the circle while the horse goes around them on the longe line. This may hold true when the horse is really good on the longe, but most of the time, you have to walk in a small "inner" circle yourself, particularly while the horse is learning or at higher speeds (fig. 2.9). So don't worry if you are moving away from the spot you started in. It doesn't mean you're doing a bad job.

The Halt-Walk-Trot Challenge

To reinforce that your horse understands all three of the basic commands, mix them up. Ask him to perform them in random order, with inconsistent requests. Do not simply let him aimlessly trot around, but ask him to speed up, slow down, halt, and then walk. The point here is to gain his attention with transitions. He should "tune" in to you because he does not know which request is coming next. If you don't "mix it up," he will soon get bored and become distracted, since all he's doing is slogging around a circle at the same pace. Young horses in particular are particularly prone to this.

Changing Direction

Now that you have the basic longe commands under control, you can tackle the slightly complicated change of direction. As I mentioned on p. 13, this manuever is best done when you are longeing with either a cavesson or halter. If you are longeing with a bridle, you must bring the horse to a halt and detach and reattach the

TROUBLESHOOTING THE HALT

Let's say you have tried the walk-halt exercise as I've described it on p. 18—consistent commands, definite movements—and the horse still does not halt for you. In such a situation, you have to be more deliberate with your "halting" hand, so that the horse better understands what you are after. When you raise the hand holding the longe line and say "Whoa," you may have to snap the line so it makes a bit of a sharp noise, as well—although only if you are working in a cavesson or halter—or even raise the horse's head with an upward thrust. Raising the head in this way facilitates the horse's hind end coming underneath his body, which in turns adds control.

If you're still having trouble, use the wall or fence of the arena or round pen. Step toward the horse's front end (see p. 18) so that your body language "pushes" the horse into the wall and encourages him to stop. Repeat. Once you get a good halt out of the horse, praise him, and then continue to ask for a halt at that same particular spot each time he goes around the longe circle. The horse learns to associate that spot with the act of halting, which gives you a natural "rhythm" of movement to rely on. When the horse halts at the same spot consistently, try the halt at different times and places. Soon, your horse will get the hang of what's expected.

longe line to the opposite side of the headstall before he can reverse.

You are now teaching a new movement, so you need to step in closer to the horse again (see p. 18). Eventually, you will be able to do the change from 10 feet away. How close should you be to begin? Close enough so the horse understands you!

Hand coordination, in particular, is very important here. If this maneuver is performed clumsily, the horse will become confused. So let's start by longeing the horse to the left. Stand in "neutral" facing the horse's "center" (see p. 22). Your left hand holds the longe line, you right hand holds your whip. Ask the horse to walk forward.

Now, to make the change of direction, reel the horse's head in toward you, and then around you to the opposite side of the circle, simultaneously switching the longe line to your right hand while switching the whip to the left (figs. 2.11 A–F). As this change is happening,

you also need to use the whip to encourage the horse's hind end to follow his head. In fact, you may need the whip as a "block" to help give direction to the horse's head if he isn't responding to your invitation to move around your position in the center of the circle. Note: Do not flick, crack, or otherwise "use" the whip near the horse's head, because this can frighten him and make him agitated. Only *present* the whip in front of him so he sees it and instinctively moves away from it. Easy enough, right?

Once you and the horse are able to change direction fluidly with you a short distance away, expand the circle until you are about 10 feet or more away—as you did in previous lessons. When the horse is changing direction on the longe line with only a subtle cue from you, you are probably close to being able to move on to more advanced longeing, such as work at the canter.

Canter

By now your horse should be able to consis-

A KEY TO LONGEING POSITIONS

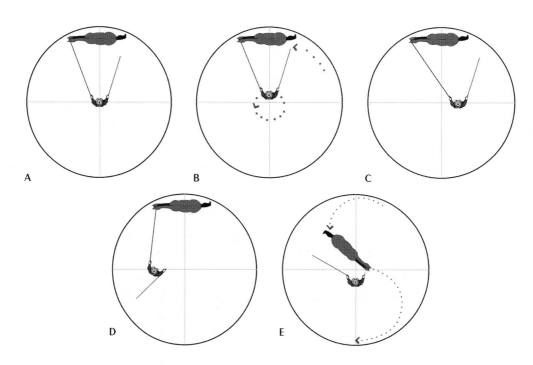

2.10   How your body is positioned affects the horse's way of going.

A   Neutral: You are the point of a triangle formed by the longe line, the horse, and the whip. This body position tells the horse to travel on as he is.

B   Many people think that when you longe your horse, you must remain stationary in the middle of the longe circle, but in fact, most of the time you have to tread a small circle of your own—especially when your horse is young or green.

C   Where you position your body helps tell your horse what you'd like him to do. Taking a step toward his hindquarters tells him to increase his pace or move forward with more impulsion.

D   Moving toward his front end tells him to slow his speed or halt.

E   When longeing in a cavesson or halter, you can teach your horse to change direction upon your command—read more about this lesson on p. 20.

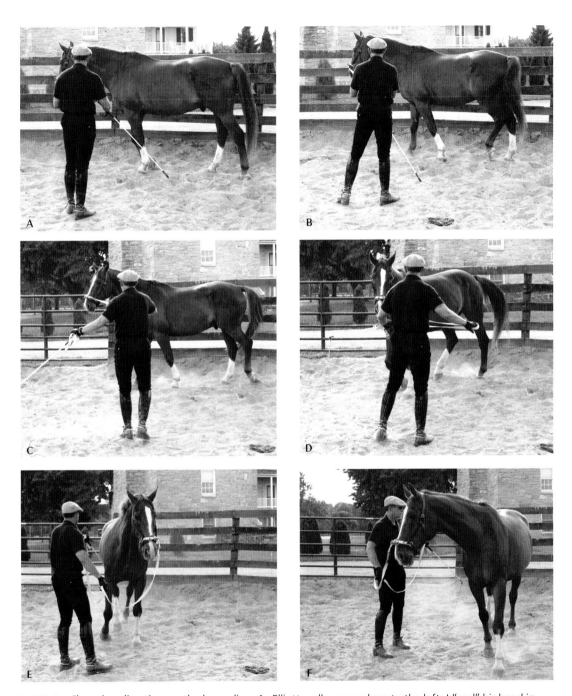

2.11 A–F Changing direction on the longe line: As Elliott walks around me to the left, I "reel" his head in toward me while simultaneously switching my longe line and whip hands (A–D). I then use the whip to help guide Elliott's hindquarters, encouraging them to follow his head around my position in the center to the opposite side of the longe circle (E & F).

2.12   I continue to "press" this horse forward at the canter with my body language—I am stepping toward his hindquarters decisively. Note his inside ear turned toward me, signaling that he is paying attention to my movements and commands.

tently perform the following on the longe line: halt, walk, up-and-down transitions, and change direction. This means you can start working on the canter. For this exercise you need to use a circle with *at least* a 15-foot longeing radius, which makes a circle the size of many round pens—about 30 feet in diameter. Eventually, your horse may be able to canter on a 60-foot diameter circle, with a 30-foot longe line extended to its full length.

Your first challenge is achieving a nice, smooth transition to the canter. Typically, the horse will do one of two things: trot faster and faster and never canter, or take off like a rocket. For the horse that simply trots faster, you must be very deliberate with your request that he change his gait, not simply speed up. Make sure you say, "Canter!" in a very upbeat way. The voice command will really help once he learns it (see more on using your voice on p. 17). If your horse takes off like a rocket when you ask him to canter, it is best to longe him in a round pen or modified arena so you have the support of a

restraining barrier (see p. 16). Many horses do this because they are unbalanced when cantering, but that does not make it acceptable. You will need to do the *opposite* of what you do with the horse that trots faster—for more about "slowing down the speed demon," see the sidebar on p. 25.

As you give the vocal cue, step toward your horse's hind end decisively as you flick the whip toward it. Even once he picks up the canter, you may have to continue "pressing" his hind end with your body language (fig. 2.12). Encourage him to hold the gait two or three times around the longe circle so he understands it wasn't a fluke but a serious request. Let him walk, then ask for the canter again, at the same place you asked him before. The horse will soon anticipate this spot as the place to canter, and he should comply easily.

Repeat this exercise using the exact same place on the longe circle each time. Then, follow the rule of being "consistently inconsistent" with your commands to make sure he is paying attention to you and not getting bored—change it up and ask for different transitions in different places.

Cantering on a longe-sized circle is difficult for some horses, so be patient. With work, the benefits of his learning to canter a small circle will pay off not only on the longe line, but under saddle as well.

Advanced Canter Work: Transitions

When your horse is truly listening to you and obedient to your requests on the longe line, change things around to keep him attentive. Mix and match transitions in all three gaits, building to the point where you can pick up the canter from a halt and come to a halt from the canter.

While you are working on these more advanced transitions, remember the horse should stand at the halt *without* turning to face you—not until you ask him to do so. If you do turn him to face you, ask him immediately to come into the circle and stand next to you for a break. Give him a good pat for a job well done.

Summary of Longeing Techniques

Here are the key points to remember when longeing:

- When starting out, never get so far away that your whip's lash cannot reach the horse. You will probably have to work on small circles during this early phase of training. That is all right.

- When longeing left (counterclockwise), the longe line is in your left hand and the whip is in your right. Reverse this when you are working the horse on the right rein.

- When you are in the "neutral" position, you form an isosceles triangle with the horse, longe line, and whip. The longe line and whip side are of equal lengths (see sidebar, p. 22).

- When you step toward the horse's head, you are in position to slow or halt the horse. By moving toward his rear end, you can create impulsion. "Pressing" the hind with your body language is often all that is required to create forward movement and impulsion.

- Do not allow too much slack in the longe line. You need light contact with the cavesson, halter, or bit. Initially, the horse may pull on you. However, as he becomes more supple and grows used to moving in a small circle, the contact will become lighter.

- Keep the whip steady. Inadvertent movements confuse the horse and send you backward in his training. Holding the whip "backward" helps to prevent this (see p. 17).

- *You* decide what the horse will do. Remember: You are longeing for a purpose. You decide the horse's pace and his gait. If he

SLOWING DOWN THE SPEED DEMON

If your horse takes off like a rocket when you give him the cue for the canter, just let him go at his own pace. As I mentioned on p. 24, it is best to longe this kind of horse in a round pen or modified arena so you have a restraining barrier to help control his speed. This way, you don't have to worry when he takes off—he isn't going anywhere, except around and around.

After he has taken a half-dozen or so strides, step toward the front of his body, raise your left hand, and attempt to transition him down to a trot. The point is to prevent him from rushing when he canters, so don't let him canter for too long. He should just barely transition up when you immediately step toward his head, raise your hand, and bring him back down. You can vary the number of canter strides you allow so the horse never knows when you are going to ask him to slow. It is important to use "enough" body language energy to get the appropriate response. Be very deliberate with your request. A wimpy one will not get you anywhere. It may require a little trial and error to see what you need to do to convince your horse to slow down. Stay patient, and praise him when he does what you have asked.

With this horse, it is usually beneficial to ask for a downward transition from the canter at the same spot on the longe circle, just as you did when teaching the halt (see sidebar, p. 21). This way, the horse begins to anticipate a downward transition and is less inclined to continue to go so fast. This forces him to think, and balance himself as he moves. Once it is clear the horse understands you and he willingly slows on cue, start mixing it up. Use different places on the longe circle to transition down. This will confirm that he is listening and responding to you.

changes gaits, especially upward, correct him immediately.

- Do not move to the next step in training until you are satisfied with the one you are working on. In other words, do not start working on the canter until the horse halts, walks, and trots on command (you can add change of direction when using a cavesson or halter), with smooth transitions up and down. If you cut corners, you will encounter setbacks, so take it slowly, and accomplish one small thing each longeing session.

- Mix things up—halt, walk, trot, canter, and direction changes—to keep your horse's attention.

- Keep the horse on the circle. Do not allow him to turn and face you or come in to the middle until you ask him. Use the tip or handle end of the whip to prod him on the shoulder or belly to send him back out if he breaks this rule.

- When the horse halts, he must stand quietly without moving. He should not swing his hindquarters in or out. This is best taught with the horse standing along the fence or wall of the arena or round pen, but eventually he should do this for you anywhere.

- If the horse pulls on you, pull back instantly, then immediately release. Repeat applying this pressure until the pulling stops. If you are positioned correctly (neutral), your pull will be lateral and very effective, as the horse is not strong laterally. By standing at the apex of the triangle (see p. 22), you have the leverage advantage.

- Remember, the goal of longe work is calmness and obedience at all three gaits and the halt, along with fluid transitions. This will make bombproofing go more smoothly, and indeed improve your general riding experience.

Long-Lining

Long-lining—that is, using two long reins to guide your horse from the ground—is a superb exercise for many reasons. When you long-line, the horse is outfitted in a bridle and snaffle bit, so consequently, it is the single best way to simulate riding under saddle while you stay safely on the ground. This can be very valuable during bombproof training. If you add side reins, this exercise teaches the horse to flex his poll, stretch down, and "give" to the bit. It also works wonderfully for bending and stretching your horse on the circle. It prevents a horse's stiff side from "falling in" on a circle and "motor biking"—that is, the horse ducking in with his inside shoulder.

You can do much more with long lines than you can with conventional longeing in the bridle because you have the added benefit of being able to change direction on the circle as much as you like, just as you would if you were on horseback.

Long-Lining Equipment

I recommend using actual "long lines" and not just two longe lines. A long line is usually manufactured so the section that runs up to the bit is narrower than the rest, thus tapering at one end. Proper long lines can also be buckled together, so you can fashion them into a continuous loop if you like. This helps prevent accidentally dropping one, losing it altogether, and the horse running off without direction.

I like using a saddle when long-lining. Leave the stirrups down as though you were sitting in it. Take a spare stirrup leather and run it through one stirrup, under the horse's belly, through the stirrup on the opposite side, and buckle it. Then run each long line through a stirrup and attach to the corresponding bit ring. Attached this way, the stirrups assist you, pro-

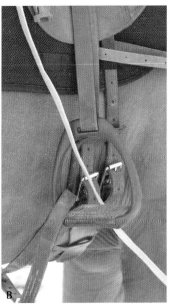

2.13 A & B   Elliott is properly turned out for a long-lining session (A). The bridle reins are secured around his neck so they will not get in the way, and the side reins are properly adjusted (see p. 14 for more on side rein use). I like to use a saddle while long-lining. I run the stirrups down on both sides and connect them under the horse's belly with an extra stirrup leather. I can then run one long line through each stirrup (B). This setup helps me control the lines and provides added leverage to mimic the rein action under saddle.

viding the leverage you need to mimic the rein action you have when riding (figs. 2.13 A & B).

Introducing Long-Lining

The first time you long-line a horse, it is best done in a round pen (you can modify your rectangular arena if necessary—see p. 16). You need the support of a fence or wall to keep the horse in a circle. In an open arena the horse can run anywhere, dragging you behind him. Enlist an assistant to stand at the horse's head and send him off on the right foot.

Let's say you are on the left side of the horse, which means that the inside line (the one that will be on the "inside" of your circle) is in your left hand. Pick up the outside line in your right hand. It should be draped over the saddle, or over the horse's hind end just behind the cantle of your saddle. Your right hand should also hold your whip or Handy Stick. As with longeing, I prefer to hold the whip in the "backward" position unless I need it (see p. 16).

To begin the exercise, you need to get the outside line down around the horse's back legs, just above the hocks. Have your assistant walk the horse in a small circle, leading him just as she would if she were walking him from his stall to his paddock, or anywhere else, so that everything feels familiar to him. Once he is moving forward nicely, have the assistant step away. Then, lightly "flip" the outside line until it goes over your horse's rump and around his hind end (figs. 2.14 A & B). This is the moment when some horses panic and attempt to run away, which is why the round pen comes in handy.

Most of the time, the horse will settle down and realize that it is no big deal, so let him run a little if he needs to. This is only his natural flight response kicking in, and he is busy assessing the situation while running. In a round pen, he will settle quickly because he is in a small area which makes it hard work to run.

2.14 A & B Anne walks at Elliott's head as I get into position. The outside long line is draped over the saddle as we begin moving forward (A). I ask Anne to step away and I "flip" the outside line over Elliott's hindquarters so it is positioned just above his hocks (B). The fence line helps guide him as he grows accustomed to the feel of the lines against his body. Note that my whip is pointed backward, in the "off" position.

Working on the Long Lines

Once your horse is comfortable with the introductory phase, you can start to work on a circle. As when longeing (see p. 11), you need to stay close to your horse at the beginning. Walk behind him, slightly to the inside of the circle. Begin with the walk, halt, and change of direction. Coordinate the vocal commands your horse learned on the longe line with your rein and whip aids (figs. 2.15 A–E). Remember that inadvertent movements on your part will cause your hands—including the whip—to signal the horse. So it is important to keep your hands quiet, just as do when you ride. Even though I

2.15 A–E   Elliott is trotting nicely to the left (A). I slow him to a walk and ask him to change direction, guiding him across the circle to the opposite side, then increasing pressure on the right rein (B & C). As he turns in the new direction I must switch the whip from my right hand to my left hand, and we pick up the trot again (D & E).

typically carry my whip pointing backward (as I mentioned earlier), when I am working with an especially lazy or stubborn horse, I may hold the whip in the more commonly seen position in front of me in order to encourage the horse to step along with every stride. Once the horse learns to long-line, you can often just leave the

2.16   Elliott canters nicely on the long lines. I've flexed him slightly toward the inside of the circle.

LONG LINES AND SIDE REINS

When you decide to use side reins with the long lines, be cautious. Your horse should be introduced to the side reins on the longe line first, as the more confined situation of longeing allows him to adjust to the feeling while you have a certain amount of control. When you add them to your long-lining lesson, remember to stay quiet and careful with your hands as you work. Using side reins with long lines will offer the same benefits as they do on the longe, but it is important to use them in an educated manner.

whip out of the equation, but it's an important tool at first.

When you first ask for the trot, keep your lines short—10 to 15 feet. You may need to "trot" along with your horse at first. Once you are both comfortable at this gait and can manage upward and downward transitions and direction changes, move on to the canter (fig. 2.16). Your distance from the horse at this gait is established by his speed; obviously, for him to canter, you need to allow him more room to maneuver, which means you are farther away. Take it slow and use the cues you taught him on the longe line (see p. 21). As the horse grows confident at the canter on the long lines, ask him to flex to the inside of the circle, while holding your outside rein steady. This is the beginning of asking him to go on the bit.

2.17 I bring Elliott in onto a smaller circle around me, asking him for more bend to the inside. When circling left, this helps stretch his muscles on the right side.

Just as you did when longeing, keep things interesting for your horse and vary the gaits and transitions you ask for. This always makes for a more alert and attentive student. As you work, bring the horse in onto a smaller circle, and then send him back out onto a larger one. You can also easily do this "spiraling" exercise because the outside long line wraps around the horse, guiding him toward you (fig. 2.17). Making a tight circle helps to stretch the horse's muscles on the outside of the circle. This is a really good option for schooling one-sided, unbalanced horses. If you work the horse's stiff side longer than his good supple side, eventually, they may even out.

Long-Lining through Obstacles

Once your horse can long-line well on the circle, you can change your position slightly and "drive" him from behind—an excellent exercise for a horse that is apprehensive about things at his rear. This enables you to guide him through an obstacle course. If he can conquer an obstacle course with you on the ground, he will be more confident when you ask him to perform a similar task under saddle (figs. 2.18 A–D). Long-lining is of great value. Not only do we use it for training young police mounts (figs. 2.19 A–C), but many people who participate in carriage driving, for pleasure or competition, use it, too. This translates directly to the work they do when the horse is actually harnessed and between the shafts (figs. 2.20 A & B).

2.18 A–D   I long-line Elliott through an obstacle course consisting of a lawn umbrella (A), a tarp (B), and hanging streamers, which he doesn't hesitate to go through (C & D). The long lines allow me to accustom Elliott to "scary" scenarios and deal with his reactions while I am on the ground, rather than in the saddle.

2.19 A–C   Young or inexperienced police mounts are often long-lined around or near obstacles in order to build their confidence. This horse is so comfortable with the drill, he "conquers" the wall of barrels with one hoof!

2.20 A & B   Noted driving-horse trainers Wilma and Martin van Hekken of the Netherlands (www.hetpaniekvrijepaard.nl) have incorporated bombproofing in their training regimens. Not only do they long-line their horses, but they actually drive them through obstacle courses, as well. Here they are in action.

2.21   The last run of Barney, Gene, and Tom, DC Fire Department horses, June, 15, 1925.

FIRE HORSE TOM

I would like to share the story of a horse named Tom who was the last "fire horse" in Washington, DC. Tom's heroic career demonstrates the importance of sane, dependable, responsive driving at a time when people depended upon horses to keep their homes intact and their loved ones safe. The story has great personal meaning to me, since Tom was named for my great-grandfather, Thomas Buckley, who was a member of the DC Fire Department.

Not every horse could serve as a fire horse. They had to live at the station, often stabled with a bit in their mouth in order to be ready to run at the sound of the alarm. They had to be strong, swift, and agile, and

yet quiet enough to stand in the face of a blaze while firefighters fought the flames and embers around them. They were remarkable examples of how brave and bombproof horses can improve the lives of the humans—in more ways than one.

Horse-drawn fire engines were eventually replaced by the motorized sort we are familiar with today, and DC's last fire horse and his "team"—Tom, Barney, and Gene—made their final ceremonial run in 1925 (fig. 2.21). Tom was retired "to pasture" where he lived 12 more years. Upon his passing, a monument was erected in his memory, engraved with, "In Memory of Tom, Last Horse in the D.C.F.D."

3

Schooling under Saddle

Introduction

A friend of mine once attended one of my bombproofing clinics, and he and his horse had some trouble negotiating a ground obstacle. I recommended that he dismount and work the horse from the ground before continuing. He said to me, "If I want something to walk around on a leash, I'll get a dog." (He's always good for a smart answer.) I laughed and left him to work it out on his own.

Even though I am a strong believer in groundwork, my friend's cheeky remark raised a valid point. It is possible that if you spend all your time on the ground and do very little schooling under saddle, you will then tend to encounter difficulty every time you ride. And, if you're reading this book, you're probably trying to improve the way your horse behaves when

you're actually riding him, not just when you work with him from the ground. You want to make him braver and more "user-friendly" under saddle, right? Well, schooling your horse in *the basics* (see below) helps to achieve these goals by making your horse easier to ride and more compliant under saddle.

The Basics

Schooling under saddle "installs" the controls you need to get the desired response from your horse. Although I discussed much of this in *Bombproof Your Horse*, I am going to expand on these skills in this book in order to give you more tools with which to handle tough situations.

I have assembled various exercises here—some from dressage and others from Western riding—to comprise a list of skills I feel every riding horse should have. Any horse and rider team should be able to manage these exercises—it doesn't matter which discipline you favor or what breed of horse you ride. Those on gaited horses can walk rather than trot through the maneuvers.

In dressage, you desire the ability to walk, trot, and canter, while achieving rhythm, impulsion, straightness, willingness, and balance. I discuss the discipline of dressage and related terms in more detail on pp. 44 and 46. In the meantime, here are the other five "dressage moves" I believe every good riding horse requires:

- Leg-yield
- Shoulder-in
- Rein-back
- Turn on the forehand
- Turn on the haunches

I also believe every horse should be able to execute the following two "Western skills":

- Side-pass
- Neck-rein

Dressage

The term "dressage" is derived from the French word *dresser*, meaning "to train" or "to prepare." The discipline was originally developed as a way to ready the horse for combat and make him obedient and maneuverable in battle. Xenophon, the famous Greek commander and horse trainer (born around 430 BC), recorded accounts of suppling and collecting exericises performed with this very purpose in mind in his famous book *The Art of Horsemanship*. Today, dressage is one of the Olympic equestrian disciplines, and its wide-ranging applications resonate with all sorts of riders. I'm not, however, trying to trick you into pursuing formal dressage training. I am just calling attention to the fact that dressage is simply a name for the basics of improving a

horse's way of going for *all* disciplines. And this includes bombproofing.

The United States Dressage Federation (USDF) says that the purpose of dressage is "to develop the horse's natural athletic ability and willingness to work making him calm, supple, and attentive to his rider." We all want a "calm, supple, attentive" horse to navigate the unfamiliar with confidence and get us through those unexpected obstacles safely. These are the same basics I strive for with the police mounts I select, ride, and train. Simply put, dressage training makes for a better, more agreeable horse for patrol work. Therefore, I will discuss schooling your horse not with a dressage test in mind, but purely to improve the horse's training. Combine this with specialized bombproofing work, and you will have a greatly improved horse.

My goal is to make dressage relevant to *every* rider, no matter her skill level or that of her horse. If you are new to dressage, I hope to convince you that this method of training is a powerful tool. It will give you and your horse improved confidence in stressful situations as he grows more manageable, responsive, and obedient to the aids. If you are already an expert, the knowledge you have can be used to great advantage when you decide to undertake bombproofing work.

Western Riding

Although neck-reining is now considered by most to be a Western maneuver, it has been used for centuries by mounted cavalry, soldiers, and knights because one hand was always occupied with some type of weapon. You can see evidence of this today in the Royal Canadian Mounted Police musical ride, in which all riders carry a lance and therefore must neck-rein with the other hand. And I spent a month in the United Kingdom studying jousting and neck-reined 90 percent of the time. If you ride English only, I hope you will find that neck-reining is useful. And, if you ride Western, I hope you will also learn the advantages of riding with two hands on occasion.

The side-pass is invaluable in any mount, especially one that ventures out on the trail. With safety and maneuverability in mind, this skill is a necessity.

Charting the Team Effort

There are 32 football teams in the National Football League. They have different coaches, playbooks, and philosophies; basically, there is more than one way to score a touchdown. But, the fundamentals are the most important part of learning the game and becoming a competitive team. Players must strive to become experts in the basics: punt, pass, kick, block, and tackle. In the same way, I am advocating that you improve your horse-and-rider team by both of you strengthening your fundamentals. First, you need to see how you score when specific skills are considered.

Create a chart, and number the horizontal axis "0" through "9," and the vertical axis "0" through "9." The "0" represents "no schooling," while the "9" indicates great experience either in or under saddle. Determine where your horse ranks, and where you rank—the amount of chart shaded in shows your combined "team experience," which can give you a pretty good visual of how prepared you might be to face day-to-day challenges in the saddle. Here are some examples:

Scenario 1: Experienced Rider/ Average Horse
The horse in 3.1 A has average schooling and benefits from an experienced rider. The rider's skills will boost the horse's performance. The

team is "weighted" toward the rider's side, but fairly capable of handling a challenge.

Scenario 2: Beginner Rider/ Experienced Horse
The example in 3.1 B is a very good "team" effort, weighted toward the horse's experience. A new rider always learns best on a "school-master," who not only serves as a teacher, but can be trusted to take good care of his rider in potentially stressful situations.

Scenario 3: Experienced Rider/ Experienced Horse
The "perfect" team is shown in 3.1 C—both horse and rider have a wealth of experience and knowledge, and make a confident and capable pair.

Create another chart, again numbered "0" to "9" on the vertical and horizontal axes. This time, the vertical axis indicates how "bombproof" your horse is, and the horizontal axis measures the amount of schooling in the basics you've undergone. Again, here are a few samples:

Scenario 1: Ticking Time Bomb!
This is not a good situation! The horse in 3.2 A is skittish, the rider inexperienced, and both have little schooling under their belt. These combined ingredients mixed with a stressful or frightening situation could have disastrous results. The horse is likely to react, the rider is not likely to handle the reaction well, and on top of it all, the unschooled horse won't listen to the aids, even if the correct ones are given.

Scenario 2: Not-So-Bombproof but Well Schooled
In 3.2 B we have an example where the rider's experience and the horse's level of schooling help make up for the fact that the horse is not yet very "bombproof." This chart demonstrates

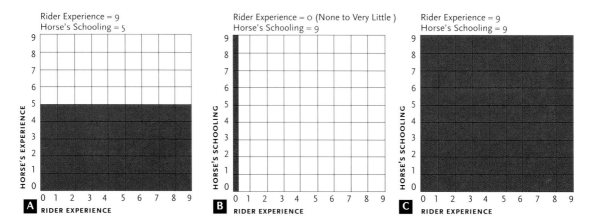

3.1 A–C   A simple chart can help you determine your and your horse's combined "team experience."

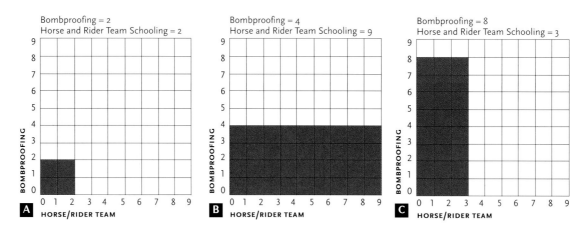

3.2 A–C Another chart helps you visualize the impact of your horse's schooling on his ability to handle new challenges and situations.

how schooling in the basics is actually *more* important than bombproofing work—because the rider knows how to handle stressful situations, and because the horse is trained to obediently and immediately respond to the aids, they are likely to handle most anything.

Scenario 3: Simply Bombproof

The chart in 3.2 C shows a very bombproof horse, whose sanity and dependability outweigh the deficiencies in his general schooling and in the rider's ability.

This formula is obviously not meant to be an exact science. It is merely to illustrate the point that bombproofing is a team effort where rider input is of great importance because the horse's ability to react to the rider's request is paramount. I hope this helps convince you to make schooling a part of your regular training. I hear people say, "Dressage is boring," all the time. I, however, like to see a horse improve, and it is a good feeling to see how much better your horse goes after just one month of work on the basics I named at the beginning of this chapter. Little improvements give you a sense of accomplishment and the incentive to continue working (fig. 3.3).

Getting a Start on Schooling

So let's begin with the most basic of dressage requirements.

Walk On

When I look at a police horse prospect, I always tell the owner that I want to see the horse ridden at the walk, trot, and canter. Seems like a pretty easy request to honor, right? Not really. You would think the walk is a given, but it isn't. I recently looked at a horse that could not walk in a straight line, could not walk more than 10 or so strides without stopping, and could not maintain rhythm in the gait. Naturally, the trot and canter were pretty bad, too.

For those of you who have ridden a dressage test, you can probably attest to the fact that the "free walk" can often be one of the most difficult movements, since it's easy for the horse to drift off track. When you let him stretch down with his head and neck, he may lose his forward "swing." A police horse I ride named Diesel tends to start jigging when you ask him to take a longer walk step. He breaks into a little trot, and won't keep a straight line.

3.3 Alanna and Yogi are happily working together. Study and application of basic dressage movements has helped them attain this pleasing picture.

The walk is *the* primary gait for police patrol. We can't trot and canter around for eight hours a day. It is important for our horses to have a nice, rhythmic walk with enough "oomph" to get where we are going (fig. 3.4). Trail riders should appreciate this as well, since there is nothing more annoying than a horse that plods along at the walk and at the slightest request for more energy, starts trotting. This is particularly true when riding with other horses. When the plodder can't keep up, the ride becomes nothing more than a series of slow walk-trot transitions, and that "gets old real quick" (fig. 3.5).

You can improve your horse's walk by paying attention to how he moves not only at the walk, but also at the trot and canter, and by recognizing how you need to sit to accommodate each gait. For the walk, notice how one of your hips or the other drops slightly as the horse's hind legs move forward. The moment your hip

3.4   You can tell even in this still photograph that Karen's horse is walking forward with good energy and rhythm.

3.5   Here a group of two-year-olds learn how to ride in a group along the busy road that runs in front of the police station. It is important that police mounts walk forward with energy, and don't dawdle, pause, or plod. A horse with these issues can be problematic when ridden in groups or in formation, and a "slowpoke" never gets where he needs to go.

drops is when you should apply a little more leg pressure with the corresponding leg *only*, so to encourage the horse to step forward a little more with that hind leg. This translates into *alternating* leg pressure. Too many times, riders try to get the horse to walk faster by applying leg pressure to both sides of the horse. That, of course, is a signal for the horse to trot, and he usually will.

Long and Low
Long and low—sometimes called "forward and down" or "showing the horse the ground"—is basically a stretching exercise to perform while riding. The point is to create a stretch along your horse's neck and topline, bringing his head down and forward as he moves (fig. 3.6). This not only activates the back muscles but also engages the horse's hind end, resulting in more impulsion. This is the basis for the horse to go "on the bit," as dressage riders call it (fig. 3.7).

How does this benefit you as it relates to bombproofing your horse? Imagine an excited, nervous horse. What does he do? His head goes up in the air, and his back hollows out and stiffens. Which would you prefer under stress, a horse with his head down, his nose near the ground, and his back supple, or one with a high head and stiff back? Well, if your horse is used to going long and low through repeated schooling, you will actually be able to use the technique in times of stress. When the horse must confront something he is not sure of, invite his nose down-and-out, and this, in turn, will offer you more control and balance.

Alleviating Anxiety

You may know of some "goofy" dressage horse that is out of control whenever he is ridden outside of the arena—specifically, the arena with which he is familiar. I have seen that situation, too. I have also noticed his frightened rider typically reacts with a "hold on and hope for the best" approach, rather than trying to employ "long and low." This doesn't work, and it teaches the horse bad habits.

As soon as you sense anxiety such as what I've described, you have to put the horse to work. Ask him to do something other than just "freak out." Substitute a *desired* behavior for an *undesired* behavior. Going long and low is a good way to divert his attention and build his confidence by giving him something he can handle.

Flex that Poll

Suppose you have no room to school or to do a nice long-and-low circle. To get your horse to go on the bit when you have no space in which to work, ask him to "give" to your hands and flex at the poll. This relaxes the muscles along the crest and topline, and helps calm him.

What's the difference between *flexing* and *bending*? *Flexion* refers mainly to the poll and its ability to move longitudinally (up and down) and laterally (left and right). When we say "flex at the poll," we are generally referring to *longitudinal* flexion. *Bend* refers to the horse's ability to flex his body from poll to tail either left or right. For example, when a horse travels the arc of a circle correctly, he is bending.

More about bending later—I like to ask a horse to flex his poll even while he is standing still. When we line up for crowd control and are standing with the officers "boot to boot," staying quiet and motionless can often be a challenge for the horse. So, I ask him to flex his poll and drop his head. This maneuver goes a long way to help relax your horse in

3.6   You can use side reins to invite your horse to go long and low, as Alanna is doing with Yogi. You must be sure they are adjusted so that the horse has room to reach forward and down.

3.7   "On the bit" means the horse has a "round" profile, yields to the reins, responds willingly to the aids, and steps under his body actively with his hind end. Yogi demonstrates a nice moment here.

MORE DRESSAGE TERMS YOU MIGHT WANT TO KNOW

These definitions will help you comprehend some of the exercises I describe in this chapter, as well as the ways in which dressage assists every horse's training. (You can find these and other dressage tips and terms in Jane Savoie's *Cross-Train Your Horse*.)

➤ On the Bit: The horse moves actively from behind through a supple back and accepts a light contact of the rein with no resistance. He yields in the jaw and poll to the rider's hand, has a "round" outline, and willingly responds to the rider's aids.

➤ Collection: Also called self-carriage or "gathered together." The horse's hindquarters lower to carry more weight; the forehand lightens and appears higher than the hindquarters.

➤ "Inside" and Outside": *Inside* refers to the direction or side toward which a horse is flexed and bent. *Outside* is the side of the horse's body that is opposite from the direction toward which he is flexed or bent. In this context the terms do not refer to the middle (center) of the arena or outside fence or wall.

a confined circumstance. Is it perfect? Does it work 100 percent of the time? Certainly not. Nothing does, when it comes to horses. However, poll flexion works very well, and often gives you an edge in managing your horse when he is under stress (fig. 3.8).

How do you get the horse to flex at the poll? I have found it easiest to teach the horse

from the trot in an arena that allows ample space for schooling. First, ride the horse in a 20-meter (approximately 60-foot) circle, or thereabouts. Pick up contact with both reins.

The *outside* rein (see sidebar, left) acts as support, and keeps the horse from drifting out. The outside rein should remain as steady and unchanging as possible. If your horse has a habit of flinging his head around and you have a hard time staying with him, use either a neck strap or breastplate to steady your hand. During this exercise, think of the outside rein as a sort of side rein—that is, it should be fixed in one place. Only relinquish it and give it to the horse when he stretches down for the bit, but even then you must maintain contact.

Ask for flexion with the *inside* rein in conjunction with using your inside lower leg to ask the horse to bend. This is not asking the horse to turn—it's simply a request for his head to "look" to the inside of the circle—slightly (fig. 3.9).

How much leg pressure should you apply as you trot, and how long do you keep it going? Just enough! You have to use just enough to *begin* to get a response. You must be able to feel that the horse is "giving" to you and trying to lower his head, and at that moment you must release and let him stretch forward and down. Praise him. When his head comes up, encourage bend around your lower leg, and ask for flexion with the hand. Then release. Keep your reins loose enough that you can give your horse whatever length he asks for, but at the same time, don't throw the reins away.

The "Required" Movements

Remember those five dressage and two Western riding maneuvers I mentioned should be required for all riding horses? It's time to get serious about them.

3.8 I ask Guy to flex his poll at the halt. This helps relax him and gives him something to do in a stressful or confined scenario.

3.9 Anne bends Elliott around her lower leg.

Leg-Yield

The *leg-yield* is a lateral movement performed in either direction, in which the horse moves both forward and sideways, crossing his legs while maintaining his impulsion. It provides a base for other lateral movements, which are good exercises for relaxing your horse and gaining his attention. In general, many lateral movements—the ones we are talking about here are leg-yield, shoulder-in, and any other movement requiring the horse's legs to cross—are often loosely referred to as "two-track" movements because you are going both forward and sideways at the same time ("single track" is just going straight forward). In actuality, a leg-yield is on *four tracks*, each leg on a separate track, while a shoulder-in is on *three tracks* (inside fore is on the first track, the outside fore and inside hind are on the second track, and the outside hind is on the third track—see p. 49 for more on shoulder-in).

Uses

Think of lateral movements such as leg-yield and shoulder-in this way: When your horse is under stress, jigging, and worried about a horse-eating monster off to his side somewhere, using a lateral movement will focus his attention more on where his feet are and less on where the perceived threat is lurking. The concentration required for him to execute these movements can help calm him down.

Aids

- ➤ The inside leg (see sidebar, p. 44, for clarification on what "inside" means) is slightly behind the girth.
- ➤ The inside rein is used to support and help create the bend, and the inside hand should be soft and giving
- ➤ The inside rein can also exert a slight upward pressure to encourage the hind end to move over, if you are experiencing

RHYTHM, IMPULSION, AND STRAIGHTNESS

Let's discuss the three qualities you are striving for in all gaits: *rhythm, impulsion,* and *straightness.*

All three are interrelated and have a profound effect on each other. When your horse achieves these qualities, his gaits are much more pleasant to ride. He also goes quietly and in a relaxed manner, which makes you more able to gain control should stressful conditions arise (fig. 3.10).

3.10 When navigating through or around obstacles, like this horse-and-rider team, it helps if the horse is moving forward with *rhythm*, *impulsion,* and *straightness.* Not only do these three qualities make for smoother gaits and a better ride, but they help ensure the horse is focused, steady, and moving forward, even when confronting the strange or unknown.

Rhythm

Rhythm is the steadiness and "sameness" of each gait. At the walk, your horse's even footfalls should almost be able to keep time with a song.

Impulsion

The next part is *impulsion*—that is, how well the horse engages his hind end. This regulates his speed and his consistency. The horse should use his haunches to "spring" into each step, creating a sense of energy in all gaits.

Straightness

Finally, we have *straightness*, which is the ability of the horse to make a straight line; or, more importantly, make a "straight circle." This has to do with his balance. On a straight line, the horse should remain straight. When on a circle, he should bend his body in the line of motion, and his hind feet should step into the tracks of his front as he goes (fig. 3.11).

I am currently schooling a young ex-racehorse. When I attempt a 20-meter circle with him, he has the tendency to run out of the circle every time he nears the outgate of the arena because he is trying to convince me we are done. It can be very difficult to make a circle when the horse insists on making something more resembling a teardrop. The inability to make a "straight circle" interrupts the rhythm and the impulsion of the horse's work.

3.11 Here I am trotting my student's horse, Yogi, on a "straight circle." Yogi is flexed at the poll, bent slightly around my inside leg, and stepping under himself nicely in a steady two-beat trot.

B

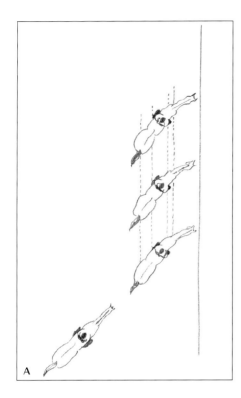

A

3.12 A & B   This illustration depicts leg yield along the wall showing four tracks (A). I then demonstrate the movement on Guy (B).

resistance either to the leg or whip. (If the horse's hind end is too far over, check your inside hand first, then correct with an open—or "leading"—outside rein. This rein aid moves *away* from the horse's neck, so an open outside rein moves away from the horse and toward the outside of the bend.)

- The outside seat bone is weighted to maintain forward impulsion.
- The outside lower leg is at the girth to help maintain forward impulsion.
- The outside rein prevents overbending by placing it at or just over the horse's withers.

While leg-yielding, the horse should have just enough bend through his body so the rider can see his inside eye. Too much bend allows the horse to duck in and evade the aids, which hinders forward impulsion.

Ways to Teach and Practice

There are many ways to train your horse to leg-yield correctly. One way is against a wall or fence (figs. 3.12 A & B). For this, the horse moves along the wall with his body at about a 45-degree angle to it, on four tracks as described earlier. It is the angle that differentiates this move from other lateral movements, such as the Western side-pass, which is ridden at an angle 90 degrees from the wall, (i.e., the horse moves sideways only) and the shoulder-in, (about 30 to 35 degrees from the wall).

One of my favorites for starting a horse unfamiliar with lateral movements is simply to walk a circle on a small circumference, but only as small as he can walk with rhythm and forward energy. Apply pressure with your inside leg as the horse steps forward with his inside hind leg. Use a dressage whip to reinforce your leg aids if necessary. If you can't feel or see the horse stepping forward (and it can be difficult, depending upon your horse), have a ground person help you by calling it out "Step, step, step," as he brings his inside hind forward.

REIN EFFECTS

1   The *direct* rein follows an imaginary line from the hand directly to the hip.
2   The *indirect* rein follows a line from the hand to the opposite hip.
3   The *opening* rein involves moving the hand sideways, away from the horse's neck. It "leads" the horse in a direction.

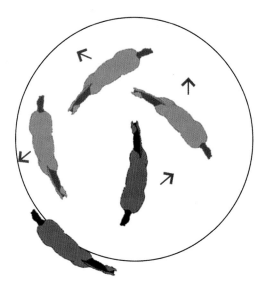

3.13   Leg-yielding out from a small to large circle.

Your goal is to leg-yield him out of the small circle, expanding it to about 20 meters (fig. 3.13). Then spiral back in on a regular series of progressively smaller circles, and repeat. Once your horse does this well, try leg-yielding both out and then leg-yielding in, switching the horse's bend. (You will find that leg-yielding back in is much more difficult because the horse has to increase his concentration and execute the motion on a more confined canvas.)

You can also practice leg-yields in a circle in a corner of the arena, and then start the leg-yield along the wall or fence coming out of the corner with the horse already bent in the correct position, toward from the wall (fig. 3.14). Only take as many steps in leg-yield as you can do correctly. If it is only a couple, so be it. It's better to have a few good teaching moments than many confusing ones. Reward your horse by straightening him and riding him forward. Repeat the exercise and remember to reinforce your leg aid with a tap from a dressage whip if you don't get a response with the leg alone. Change rein and work in the other direction.

Leg-Yield Challenge
To challenge yourself and your horse, try another version of the exercise. Begin by riding

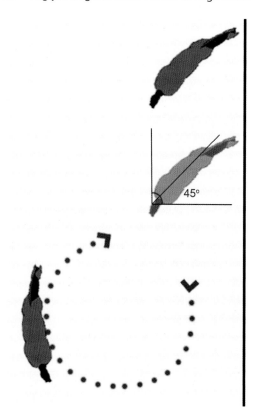

3.14   Leg-yielding out of the circle and along the wall.

around the arena on the right rein (clockwise) as you normally would, with the horse bent around your *right* leg in the corners. As you approach the second corner on the short side, straighten your horse momentarily before bending him around your *left* leg and leg-yield him down the wall at a 45-degree angle. Now, up the ante, and perform a change of direction in leg-yield in an open part of the arena. Let's say you are going to the right around the arena bent around your *right* leg. When you reach the centerline, turn down it, and keeping the horse's bend the same, leg-yield him down the centerline. After a few strides, leg-yield the horse to the left—away from the centerline—on a diagonal toward the wall. When you reach the wall, straighten him momentarily before changing the bend, then leg-yield him (now bent around your *left* leg) back to the centerline. Leg-yield down the centerline for two more strides, then across to the wall or fence on the right. Straighten before repeating the exercise again down the centerline from the opposite end of the arena (figs. 3.15 A–E).

When teaching this movement to an uneducated horse, you may have to help him by giving a little extra direction with your outside hand. Your *outside hand*—the hand opposite the side the horse is bent around—offers an open (or "leading") rein, slightly off the horse's neck. It should guide, not force, the horse—first to the left in this exercise, and then to the right. Eventually, your goal will be to stop using this open rein, which is just a means to an end to help teach the leg-yield.

Shoulder-In

As I explained early in this chapter, the *shoulder-in* is a lateral movement in which the horse's body is on three tracks at about a 30- to 35-degree angle to the line he is on (see p. 45). In the shoulder-in, the horse's shoulder is toward the center of the arena while his haunches are toward the wall or fence, and he is slightly bent around the rider's inside leg (figs. 3.16 A & B).

I touched on the shoulder-in in *Bombproof Your Horse*, but there I referred to it as "head-away." Whatever you call it, this lateral movement is very good for *proactive* riding, especially in traffic or on the trail. It is a great way to place your horse's haunches toward the threat, and his head away from it. Imagine you are riding in traffic on the right side of the road, and perceive a potential distraction—a garbage truck, two people with jogging strollers, or three kids on mopeds—ahead on your side of the street. Even though your horse may be frightened of these, you know that your bigger threat is the traffic on the left side. The shoulder-in gives you a tool to manage your horse's response, and keep him away from the real danger.

Some people will say, "Yes, but my horse wants to look at things, and it's better to let him see what it is he thinks he's afraid of." Believe me, your horse can still see perfectly well with his haunches toward the threat and his head away from it. I have nothing against a horse looking, sniffing, and assessing the situation for himself. The problem is that many horses assess things while they flee them! In situations such as the one I've just described involving traffic, I do not want my horse running into moving cars while he takes his time deciding whether or not to be afraid of the mopeds.

If you are able to get past the object(s) and the situation is such that you can safely use it as a training exercise, then go back and walk by the object(s) again until your horse is comfortable with them. Let him look and sniff all he wants. Just don't make the scenario worse by allowing the horse to disrupt traffic, run over citizens, or otherwise be a safety hazard.

3.15 A–E   For an additional challenge, practice leg-yielding across the diagonal (A). Anne and Elliott demonstrate the maneuver, with Anne using an "open" left rein to guide him (see p. 48), though still keeping him bent away from the direction of travel (B–E). When they reach the rail, Anne will change Elliott's bend and ask him to leg-yield back to the centerline.

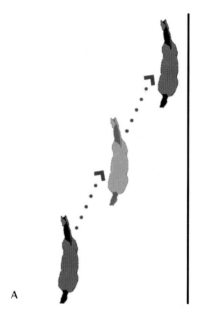

A

B

C

D

E

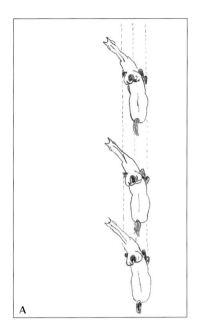

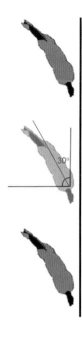

3.16 A & B The shoulder-in on three tracks (A). The horse's body should be at a 30- to 35-degree angle to his line of travel (B).

A   B

Uses

- ➤ Negotiating an obstacle on one side.
- ➤ Negotiating obstacles on both sides. Pick your horse's best side and keep impulsion at either the walk or the trot. Use shoulder-in as a distraction. He has to think of feet placement and therefore less about what is bothering him.
- ➤ Crossing something, like a creek, that the horse insists on jumping. (It is fairly difficult for horses to jump when their front feet are crossing each other.)
- ➤ General suppling (and calming) before work.

Aids

- ➤ The inside leg just behind the girth.
- ➤ The outside leg for support.
- ➤ The inside seat bone is weighted.
- ➤ The inside hand gently asks for flexion. Do not cross this hand over the withers. Feel for when your horse "gives" to you and then release. Do not overbend him. You should just see a hint of his eye or eyelash.

Ways to Teach and Practice

Begin a 10-meter, left-hand (counter-clockwise) circle at the walk in a corner. This will help even a green horse establish the correct bend for the exercise. Once you are satisfied with the bend, simply move the horse out of the circle on the long side of the wall and begin the shoulder-in by asking the horse to step well under his body each time his inside leg moves forward (fig. 3.17).

As with the leg-yield (see p. 44), if you are having timing issues, ask an assistant on the ground to tell you when the inside hind leg is stepping forward. This will help you get in a productive cycle of pushing and releasing. Don't lay, and leave, your leg on the horse, or nag him constantly because he will eventually become dead to your leg aids. Remember, you can reinforce the leg with a dressage whip if necessary.

3.17 I ask Guy for a shoulder-in along the rail. Notice how he is on three tracks as opposed to the four tracks in the leg-yield (see fig. 3.12 B, p. 47).

Rein-Back

Uses

When performing the rein-back, the horse takes steps backward in a cadenced fashion, and his feet move in a two-beat diagonal pair pattern. We mounted police use the rein-back for things like making a traffic stop, dealing with a suspect, riding in formation, and crowd control. It is needed when opening a gate. It can also be used on occasion to negotiate an obstacle—such as a puddle—that the horse resists going over forward. (Don't rely on this trick, though, because the horse may then only want to cross or go through things in reverse. Use it sparingly, and immediately transition to going over the obstacle again, but this time *forward*.) And of course, if you ever find yourself "trapped" at a "dead end" on a trail, the rein-back can help you get out of a tough spot.

Aids

Apply leg pressure and a resistant hand at the same time. The horse senses the resistance, and moves away from it, which takes him backward. You can also lighten your seat pressure in order to encourage the movement.

Troubleshooting Exercise

When you ask for the rein-back, the horse may toss his head or refuse to "give" to your hand. This sometimes confusing movement cannot be forced, so here are a couple of techniques you can use until the horse "gets it."

Sometimes a slight upward pressure on the reins encourages a shift of the horse's weight to the hindquarters and facilitates the request. Another technique is to apply just a little extra backward pressure with *one* rein. This often "unlocks" the horse's hind end, and he will step backward. He may step a little crookedly, but that is all right, as long as he steps to the rear and does not execute a partial turn on the forehand (see p. 53).

If you are still struggling after trying these two methods, then it may be best to teach your horse the rein-back from the ground. Stand at your horse's head, apply rein pressure and ask your horse to back up. A little pressure with the butt end of the dressage whip on his chest may help. Then, try again from the saddle with a ground person to assist you. However, be sure she does not "push" your horse backward, but simply supports the aids you are already giving him.

The rein-back is often accompanied by problems such as crookedness, rushing backward, or a lack of adequate energy in the movement. All of these faults can be fixed with patience and progressive training, and they typically resolve quickly once the horse understands the aids. So, don't worry about them in the early stages of training, just work on getting the communication right with your horse.

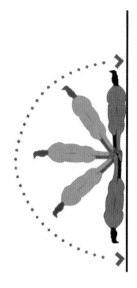

A   B

3.18 A & B   The turn on the forehand involves the horse moving his hindquarters 180 degrees around his forehand, which remains in the same spot (A). When first learning the movement, it may be easier for the horse to move his front feet in a small half-circle, rather than pivot in place (B).

Turn on the Forehand

In a *turn on the forehand,* the horse learns to move away from the rider's leg when he is at a standstill. His front legs remain in one spot while his hindquarters make a 180-degree turn around his forehand. Learning this movement teaches a horse to respond to the rider's sideways-pushing aids. When first learning, it is often easier for the horse to step a smaller circle with his front feet rather than keep them on one spot (figs. 3.18 A & B).

Some dressage riders prefer to avoid the turn on the forehand because the horse's gravity gets shifted to the front legs and their entire goal in training is to get the horse's weight *off* his forehand and to carry it increasingly from the rear end. However, I feel the move has great practical value.

Uses

Applications for the turn on the forehand include opening gates. Mounted police officers use a turn on the forehand during traffic stops, when dealing with suspects, and for crowd control. It is also a great "distraction" device

when you anticipate your horse is about to do something adverse. Put him to work by getting his head down and his feet moving with a turn on the forehand.

Aids

To teach a horse the turn on the forehand, face a wall or a fence. This helps keep the horse from stepping forward. To move his haunches to the right, place your left leg slightly behind the girth and apply pressure while flexing the horse's head slightly to the the left. If you get no response with your leg, you can tap with a dressage whip or gently apply your spurs. If you still get no response, apply a slight amount of upward pressure on the left rein as you turn the horse's head. This upward pressure helps to move his hind end over. Only ask your horse to take a couple of steps at a time.

Troubleshooting Exercise

If you're having trouble with this movement and your horse just doesn't "get it," try the following exercise, which is very good for teaching a horse that will not perform a turn on the

3.19 A & B By "walking into" the turn on the forehand, you can help the horse "get it," as the impulsion from the forward motion helps disengage his hind end and swing it around in response to your leg aid (A). At first, the horse's front feet may move in a small half-circle, rather than remain in place around a single pivot point as is ideal (B).

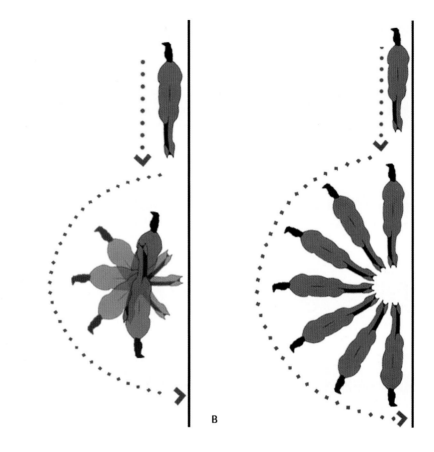

A

B

forehand. It can also help with leg-yielding, and sets the foundation for other lateral movements as well (see p. 44).

Ride at a walk counterclockwise along the wall or fence with a dressage whip in your right hand Once you establish enough impulsion, turn the horse's head to the wall while simultaneously applying pressure behind the girth with your right leg or with your whip. The horse will describe a small arc with his front feet and a larger one with his hind feet. With his head turned like this, the horse should at least take a couple of steps to the left with his hind legs crossing. This is a partial turn on the forehand, so halt and praise him so he understands what

you want from him. Your goal is to ride one or two good steps with the horse disengaging his hind end (figs. 3.19 A & B).

Now face the opposite direction, with the wall on your left side. Switch the hand holding the whip, and walk back along the wall, performing the same exercise from the new direction (figs. 3.20 A–F). Practice this daily, for no longer than 10 minutes, until the horse improves. The impulsion gained from doing this exercise at a walk helps to unlock the horse's hind end and facilitates his ability to eventually perform it from a standstill and in the center of the arena without a prop like the wall or fence.

3.20 A–F Guy and I "walk into" a turn on the forehand along the fence line. Guy's impulsion facilitates the movement. Notice that at this stage his front feet describe a small semi-circle. As he progresses, he will learn to turn on the spot, pivoting on one leg.

HALF-HALT

A *half-halt* sounds as if you are "half" asking your horse to stop. It's not quite that but rather a coordinated action of seat, legs, and hands that rebalances the horse and gains his attention.

the horse's energy should be poured into his turn. You can perform a turn on the haunches from a walk or a halt, although—as with the turn on the forehand (see p. 53)—when you are first teaching the movement, it is often easier for him to do it from a walk.

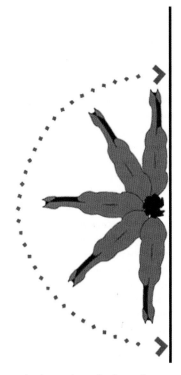

3.21 In the turn on the haunches, the horse's forehand moves 180 degrees around his hindquarters, with the inside hind foot as a pivot point.

Turn on the Haunches

Uses

The turn on the haunches is a great exercise for engaging the horse's hindquarters and encouraging good flexion of the joints in the hind end, which will help improve your horse's canter departure. In the exercise, the horse's forehand moves around his hindquarters, with his outside front foot crossing over his inside front foot (fig. 3.21). The horse's inside hind leg is the pivot point—it must be picked up and put down as it remains basically in the same spot. Ideally, there is no forward or backward movement—all

Aids

For a turn on the haunches to the right:

- An inside *direct* rein, and outside *indirect* rein is applied (see below and p. 48).
- The inside leg rests against the horse's side, but is not active.
- The outside leg is positioned at the girth to direct the horse to move his front feet to the right and to generate impulsion.

Ways to Teach and Practice

The inside *direct* rein (right, in the above scenario) directs the horse into the turn and the outside *indirect* rein (left) moves the shoulders to the right and prevents the horse's head from turning too much to the right. Begin at the walk; perform a slight half-halt (see sidebar, p. 55) to gain the horse's attention and shift his weight to his rear. Be ready to make slight corrections as the horse will probably attempt to step forward as you begin the turn. Maintain impulsion, and do not to allow the horse to back up (figs. 3.22 A–H).

Once you have completed the turn, bring your hands back to a neutral position, keeping them quiet and steady throughout the maneuver. Remember, when first teaching the turn on the haunches, it may not be pretty. It's not a beginner's movement. You have to work through it gradually and accept slight improvements as milestones. Eventually, you should be able to do one in either direction from a halt.

3.22 A–H   Anne asks Elliott for a turn on the haunches along the fence line.

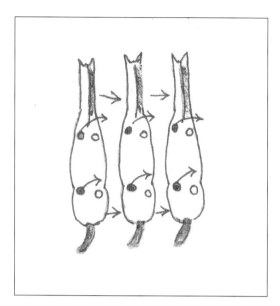

3.23 The side-pass is a purely lateral movement, with both front and hind legs crossing.

Side-Pass

The side-pass is a movement where the horse moves laterally *only*: there should be no forward motion (fig. 3.23). If your horse can do a turn on the forehand (p. 53) and leg-yield (p. 44), this movement will come easily. It is a little more difficult because you start from a halt and the horse has to resist walking forward. He is also more likely to step on himself because both his front and hind feet cross over one another, though you, of course, can always incorporate bell or galloping boots if you are concerned about this happening.

Uses

The side-pass has many practical applications in police work and on the trail. When your horse will move directly sideways at your command, you have another way to control where his body is at all times, as well as how you navigate obstacles.

Aids

To move to the right, take an *open* right rein (away from the horse's neck) to direct his front end to the right. The left rein should rest on the horse's neck, applying neck-rein pressure as needed to move the front end laterally (see below). Simultaneously, apply left leg pressure slightly behind the girth to move the hindquarters to the right.

Ways to Teach and Practice

Teach the horse to leg-yield and turn on the forehand before you attempt the side-pass. When you are ready to train the horse to do a side-pass, face the wall or fence as this barrier prevents him from trying to evade by moving forward (fig. 3.24). The object is for the horse to maintain a 90-degree angle to the wall while moving directly sideways. As you and your horse improve, attempt it with the neck-rein only.

Neck-Reining

Neck-reining is an *indirect* rein aid. You use a loose rein, laid across the horse's neck, to indicate which direction he should move. When you neck-rein, you ride one-handed.

Uses

Although all Western riders are accustomed to riding one-handed, most English riders find it unsettling. Being able to neck-rein, however, is another very practical and useful riding tool to have at your disposal, no matter what your usual riding discipline. It is virtually impossible to carry a flag effectively if your horse doesn't understand how to neck-rein. It is also useful for the ever-present gate, which is nice to open and close without dismounting and remounting every time through (see p. 81). Mounted police always seem to have something else to deal with in one of their hands—a baton, ticket book, pen, radio, microphone, firearm—so neck-reining is very useful for us.

3.24   Anne teaches Guy to side-pass along the fence, which provides a barrier to prevent him from walking forward.

3.25   It is correct to carry a flag with your right hand, on the right side of the horse. This means it is necessary for your horse to neck-rein, and for you to be able to guide him with your left hand. (Find out more about carrying flags on p. 81.)

Neck-reining offers you an additional riding skill, as well. It is best to learn to neck-rein using your weak hand, because you will naturally want to use your dominant one for most activities. For example, if you're a southpaw facing a gate, your reins will be in your right hand as your left unfastens the gate's latch. The only exception I make to this rule is when carrying a flag. This is always carried in your right hand, on the right side of the horse (fig. 3.25 and see more about carrying flags in chapter 5, p. 81).

Aids

To turn right, you lay the left rein against the left side of the horse's neck. To turn left, lay the right rein against the right side of the horse's neck.

Ways to Teach and Practice

To teach the neck-rein as you make a turn to the right: use a *direct* rein with your right hand and lay the left rein on the horse's neck. He will grow to associate the feeling of the rein lying there with the more familiar one of a gentle tug to the right. Mix your turns up as you work, neck-reining to the left next.

Do figure eights, 90-degree turns, and any other patterns you can think of, all maintaining that rein on the neck. You gradually want to wean yourself from using two hands and begin making the turns with one hand. Be ready to employ your idle hand for additional direct rein guidance as you need it (fig. 3.26). Have some slack in the rein, and keep the horse looking in the direction he is going.

A fun way to practice neck-reining is to set up a pole-bending course and walk or trot through it (fig. 3.27). The rhythmic pattern of the poles will help your horse associate the feel of the rein against his neck with the turn in the correct direction.

3.26 Anne demonstrates adding her "idle" hand (her left) to offer some opening rein guidance when training her horse to neck-rein.

3.27 Anne and Elliott have fun practicing their neck-reining through a pole-bending course. Anne's "idle" right hand is ready to help out with direct rein pressure if needed.

Schooling on the Spot

You don't always need an arena to school your horse properly. Here is one handy on-the-spot exercise that I picked up from Jerry Mayo of the Royal Canadian Mounted Police. You can perform the following exercise routine in an area as small as 10 by 10 feet:

➤ Turn on the forehand

➤ Rein-back

➤ Side-pass

➤ Walk forward to halt

➤ Turn on the haunches (Note: This is optional. It is the most difficult movement. You can have a satisfactory workout by doing the other maneuvers listed.)

Mix up these four or five movements any way you like and use them as one complete exercise for about 10 minutes at a time each day you ride, and your horse's way of going and willingness to listen to your aids will improve dramatically. Add some neck-rein practice for good measure and you have a real schooling workout.

All of the movements I've described in this chapter can be worked into your daily riding life. While walking along the trail, take some time to leg-yield from one side to the other. In fact, anytime you need to move to one side of the trail while walking, use the leg-yield instead of just turning the horse's head. You can practice the shoulder-in this way, too.

Bombproofing with the Basics

Your equitation skills and your horse's level of schooling complement one another to produce a more efficient and manageable horse. I'll summarize what I've discussed in this chapter to put it into perspective.

➤ Your horse should be *forward*. By encouraging his willingness to move forward you will prevent a lot of problems—it makes it more difficult for the horse to do something undesirable, and it also means you have your aids on the horse, thus instilling confidence in him.

➤ Use the various lateral movements to your benefit. The shoulder-in helps you ride past or over obstacles, and is a great distraction from all manner of external stimuli. Use the turn on the forehand for "on the spot" issues, such as where you have to change direction in a small space, or get close to a gate or mailbox.

➤ The rein-back can be used to negotiate certain obstacles, such as "scary" water puddles on the trail. Back the horse into the puddle and—lo and behold!—he will find himself standing in the middle of the very

thing that frightened him. (Obviously, don't use the rein-back for obstacles that the horse could trip on.)

➤ Neck-reining is very a utilitarian skill, since it is virtually impossible to do anything else from the saddle besides ride when your horse refuses to be neck-reined. Remember, though, that when the horse is under stress, you may have to put both hands on the reins, even if you usually ride Western. When your horse shies, or spins to one side, the neck-rein may not be enough to counter it. I believe that English riders need to learn to neck-rein and Western riders sometimes need to use two hands.

➤ Use the direct rein to make corrections. Think of "closing the doors." In other words, when you approach something

VARIETY: THE SPICE OF SCHOOLING

I touched upon the importance of riding different figures and patterns in *Bombproof Your Horse*. Riding a variety of patterns when schooling helps to supple your horse and add diversity to your training. Mixing things up also helps alleviate boredom that tends to accompany ring work—although, of course, sometimes you have to practice certain maneuvers in one direction before you can practice them in the other.

For example, once you are able to elicit a consistent response from your horse on a circle in both directions, start riding figure eights, then a serpentine consisting of three loops. Then mix them all together to keep it interesting.

3.28 A & B Anne schools Elliott around several obstacles. Notice Elliott's raised head showing concern and tension (A). Anne immediately puts Elliott to work, trotting him forward on the bit, and soon he is going along in a relaxed manner, even near the balloons that worried him before (B). Use schooling like this to relax your horse when he is under stress.

and the horse begins to spin left, immediately correct with the right rein to bring the horse back on task while keeping the forward driving aids on. Show the horse that the only open door is *forward*; the rest are *closed*. This, and enough confidence to push him on, may be all that is needed to negotiate the issue. Nothing is 100 percent effective, but just sitting there being a passenger while the horse runs for the barn certainly won't work.

➤ Your basic riding position is important. A commonly seen "bombproofing fault" is when a rider assumes a defensive position and "unweights" her seat. When the seat

aids come off the horse, he feels it, and it can cause him to lose confidence in his rider—he is not certain she knows what the two of them are doing and where they are going. Remember the horse gains self-assurance from you through your aids. When those aids are tentative or sporadic, he becomes concerned.

School your horse regularly and you will never be without a useful tool to use in a possibly problematic situation; you can always put him to work to gain his attention. In addition, as I've mentioned, the rhythm of familiar work is a good distraction before you ask him to under-

B

take something that may be stressful, whether a new trail or a bombproofing clinic (figs. 3.28 A & B). Relax your horse with long-and-low work; ride figures and patterns; and do lateral movements to keep his mind occupied with something positive.

Schooling these movements is useful for substituting desired behavior for undesirable behavior, and gives you a large arsenal to which to turn. For example:

- Maybe you are in a tight spot and only have room for a precise turn on the forehand.
- While at halt, ask your horse to give to the bit and flex at the poll.
- Use the shoulder-in proactively to manage a perceived threat up ahead.

Think about problems as soon as you become aware of them, so you can come up with plans to manage them. This is what makes the difference between a rider and a passenger.

4

Common Issues
that Interfere with the
Bombproofing Process

Conquering Training Troubles

At my bombproofing clinics, I encounter an array of issues that can get in the way of the development of a bombproof horse-and-rider team capable of conquering any challenge. The types of problems I see include ineffective riding and handling, herd-bound horses, and rider fear, to name a few. I don't want to classify these as "bad habits" in the same sense that rearing or bucking are bad. These problems—and others I commonly see—can generally be resolved fairly quickly so as to allow horse and rider to get the most of their bombproofing experience. But when a rearing or bucking horse is brought to one of my clinics, I tell the owner that the vice will need to be fixed before we can do any bombproofing, at all. (Note: I addressed these dangerous types of difficulties in *Bombproof Your Horse*.)

Although they may not be quite as dramatic, the following training problems must be resolved in order to move on with the bombproofing process.

Lack of Control

A general lack of control—when the rider is in the saddle or has her horse in-hand—can crop up at any moment and cause trouble. It's absolutely the most common problem I see, and it happens to one degree or another every time I teach.

At the beginning of a clinic, I first ask all of the riders to hand-walk their horses into the arena. I have all my equipment, from flares to tarps to mattresses, off to the side (nothing is set up yet), and usually I'll have some music

4.1 A & B I always have my clinic participants hand-walk their horses around the arena before we begin. This allows the horses to become accustomed to their surroundings while the rider is still safely on the ground.

playing quietly, as well. This scene, although a far cry from what they will face later in the clinic, often intimidates the horses right off. My goal is for them to settle down quickly without endangering their riders—and this is best accomplished from the ground (figs. 4.1 A & B). The riders walk around the arena at least once, and then they change direction, and only after they have circled both ways do I ask them to mount up. This introduction eases the horses into the unusual environment gradually.

Inattention on the Ground

Running Away

At this stage, and with all my paraphernalia spread about, I sometimes see a horse try to run away—bolting for the arena gate or into other people or horses. Typically, the handler responds by taking a tighter hold of the reins and leaning into her horse. This only serves to aggravate the horse more, and the handler is now in a precarious position as she tries to manage a frantic horse around many other horses and people.

My section on "Longeing with a Purpose" on p. 14 describes how to instill discipline and responsiveness on the ground, which could help improve such a situation for the future. But, when faced with the issue as it is happening, I need to get the horse's attention and calm him down. The first thing I do is to take the horse from the rider and immediately let him have his head (fig. 4.2). If he attempts to run off, I don't choke up on the reins, I simply pull him into a small circle around me as if longeing him. Then, I continue walking with the horse on his near side.

As I walk along, I hold the end of the reins in my left hand. My right hand is positioned about 6 inches from the bit, with as much slack as possible. The slack is often enough to settle the horse who no longer feels trapped as he did when there was so much pressure on the bit. If he continues to misbehave, I unbuckle the off-side rein from the bit. This gives me a ready-made longe line with the entire length of two reins available. I can put him onto a circle and start longeing.

Pushiness

When walking next to your horse on his near side, your right hand needs to always be ready to push the horse away if he is the type that has to be "in your pocket" as he walks. Usu-

4.2   When a horse gets nervous or bolts when being led, the handler's reaction is often to grab a tight hold of the reins and lean into her horse. In these situations, I take over and immediately give the horse his head.

TRAINING CHALLENGES WITH DONKEYS, BURROS, AND MULES

I do not claim to be an expert on training donkeys, burros, or mules. However, I have had some experience with them in my clinics, and I try to pick up information about them whenever I can (fig. 4.3).

Because donkeys have such strong self-preservation instincts, handling them can be challenging. In fact, riders often refer to donkeys and burros as "stubborn." But it is actually the donkey's survival instinct that makes him consider seriously what you are asking him to do. Frightening or threatening a donkey only makes the problem worse.

Donkeys, burros, and mules are trustworthy. Of course, with any equine partner you need trust in order to work together well, but these animals will offer you ten times more trust than a horse. So gaining their trust is first and foremost in training them, because once you have that, they will follow you anywhere.

4.3   A donkey going over an obstacle at one of my bombproofing clinics.

These equines appreciate reward and praise, and the process for offering these does not differ from what we use for horses. And you still have to reward the animal at the proper time—if you constantly give treats in the hopes that he will perform a specific action, you are using reverse logic. He should be rewarded only for a positive response. Don't reward him in hopes that he will do the right thing to earn it.

I have had both donkeys and mules in my bombproofing clinics. On one of these occasions, a student brought a little donkey on a lead line. He minded his own business and calmly went through all the obstacles I had set out. Meanwhile, a couple of the horses were not too happy with the donkey's presence. I started getting complaints from riders that the donkey was scaring their horses. I reminded the riders they were at a bombproofing clinic, and that they should consider the donkey as just another obstacle to overcome. That poor donkey was getting a bad rap.

4.4 A & B   Here are two examples of horses remaining in control and responsive to their riders in the face of potentially "scary" obstacles. Through proper schooling in the basics, the riders remain calm and confident, and the horses happily comply with their riders' request to go over and through the obstacles.

ally, a shove from your hand tells him to keep the proper distance, but you can also use your elbow to give yourself some space when you have an extremely pushy horse that endangers you with his lack of respect. Each time he veers in toward you as you're walking, he should run into your elbow. You didn't do anything; he did it to himself. Continue walking, quickly correcting any attempts to run off or run into you. Praise the horse with your voice and with a nice pat as soon as he is doing the right thing—in this case, walking quietly at your side. It is important to *never* pat a horse in an attempt to calm him in a "threatening" situation. Only pat him for a positive response to that situation.

This, however, is a "crash course." I can generally calm down most horses to a manageable level within about five minutes of doing what I've just described. The root of the problem—that is, the rider or handler not correcting her horse properly—still exists and must eventually be addressed for the situation to really improve.

Inattention under Saddle

A horse that is inattentive on the ground may be far more difficult to deal with once you mount up, so you need to use a combination of actions to confront this situation. First of all, as when your horse causes problems on

the ground, use longeing with a purpose as a regular part of your training program. Longeing instills respect and an understanding of the level of response expected. Then, work on the basics—the exercises I offered in chapter 3 (p. 37)—to give you the tools you need to substitute *undesired* behavior with *desired* behavior. As I've explained, when your horse has something productive to do, he is far more likely to respond to your aids and remain in control (figs. 4.4 A & B). Always remember you can dismount and work your horse in-hand should you ever feel unsafe (see p. 6).

Calming the horse while in the saddle relies upon similar techniques to calming him on the ground. I strongly believe in the power of *long and low* (see p. 42). But, let's say I'm trying to help a first-timer at a clinic, and we are looking to resolve an under-saddle issue quickly—and we're assuming the rider doesn't know how to perform long and low, and the horse doesn't either.

Loosen Your "Death Grip"

Many riders tend to take a tighter grip on the reins when confronted with a nervous or tense horse. Tight reins are the number-one mistake that causes problem behavior to escalate—it has the same effect as a tight grasp on the ground (see p. 66). Instead of choking up on the reins when your horse grows anxious, you should ride the horse in a circle at the walk. Each time the horse tries to run off, jig, or trot, give a half-halt (see p. 55) and then immediately loosen your pressure on the reins. Don't throw the reins away, but work to gradually loosen your "death grip." Your goal is to have a light contact with your horse's mouth and your reins at a medium length while the horse walks steadily in a circle without stopping (figs. 4.5 A & B).

If your circling does not ease the horse's tension and he continues to consider running away a valid option, you can vary the half-halt/release by halt-halting, then immediately taking the horse's head to the inside of the circle. Reinforce this with *inside* leg pressure to create bend in his body, and release the inside rein. The slack rein will encourage the horse to drop his head to the inside. Keep light contact with the outside rein. Repeat as necessary. Don't give up just because the exercise doesn't give you an immediate fix. Look for—and praise—any improvement from your horse, no matter how gradual or slight.

Adding Ground Poles for Control

If the horse still remains frantic or excited—even after these exercises—try to keep your requests mentally stimulating and add a ground pole to your work. Instead of a circle, now ride your horse in a figure-eight pattern. Place the pole in the center of the eight, right where your right-hand and left-hand circles join and you change direction. Continue using the half-halt to slow the horse's gait, striving to loosen the reins to a light contact. This encourages the horse to stretch his neck down (the beginnings of long and low), which calms him. The ground pole is simply there to provide a distraction: Its presence makes the horse think and gives him a clear destination that keeps him moving forward at all times. It makes the horse look where he is going and pay more attention to his feet than his anxiety (fig. 4.6).

4.5 A & B   This rider lets her horse assess the situation by giving him some rein, but she doesn't "throw them away"—she maintains contact with his mouth in case she needs it.

4.6   Karen's horse looks down as he steps over the ground pole, demonstrating the value of adding one to your patterns and figures when your horse is nervous: The horse has to pay attention to his feet, which takes his mind off the cause of his anxiety.

A

B

C

D

4.7 A–D I work Elliott over three ground poles placed in the context of a figure-eight pattern. The addition of the ground poles adds variety to the exercise and makes him think, and in a stressful situation, can help him regain his composure by subduing the flight response.

You can add further interest to the exercise if you place a ground pole on the line of each of the circles in the figure eight, as well (figs. 4.7 A–D).

Troubleshooting Anxiety under Saddle
There are many other ways to achieve your goal of occupying the mind of your horse in order to calm and focus him. Here are some to keep in your arsenal:

- The "two-track" movements I discussed in chapter 3 (see p. 37) cause your horse to "cross" his feet, so he needs to concentrate on where his feet are, and has less time to think about his fear. I like leg-yielding and shoulder-in because the horse moves forward and sideways at the same time. Keeping him moving forward helps to dissipate anxiety more than the side-pass does, which is a completely lateral movement.
- When you are standing still and the horse is only mildly inattentive or he's just starting to become concerned, put him *on the bit* and ask him to flex at the poll (see p. 43).
- When you have little room at your disposal to work your horse, do some schooling on the spot to regain his attention (see p. 60). Remember to keep him guessing about what is coming next.

The Herd-Bound Horse

This is the horse that arrives at a clinic with his

best barn buddy, then becomes unruly whenever the two of them are separated. Invariably, the two horses come to the clinic together because the owners are afraid to separate them in the first place. However, the obsession is usually one-sided: one of the horses can be persuaded to move along, while the other whinnies and misbehaves when he can't see his companion (fig. 4.8).

This is not the typical kind of herd-bound horse that I dealt with in *Bombproof Your Horse*. After all, we are now in a clinic situation with 20 to 25 horses present, so it isn't as if he is being left all alone. The horse in *this* situation insists on being right with the barn buddy at all times. He doesn't care about the other horses.

This is actually one of those long-term bad habits—like rearing and bucking—that really must be fixed before you can pursue a serious bombproofing program. Doing so will take considerable time, patience, perseverance, commitment, and consistency, both at home and during any kind of schooling or hacking. In a clinic situation, however, I tell the rider with the herd-bound horse to simply to stay with his buddy since a one-day clinic will not fix the situation, and I have twenty-odd other horse-and-rider teams to think about.

I do, however, ask the rider to make immediate and small steps toward resolving the issue. For example, during the day I'll periodically ask her to ride a short distance away from the friend, and then return. I then have the buddy horse ride away, and return. We increase the distance and the time the herd-bound horse and his buddy spend apart, making sure to always meet back up to keep everyone under control. This way, we lay the foundation for the work the rider has ahead of her, and begin to give the horse some confidence that he can survive a new situation without his buddy by his side.

4.8 An Asbury Police Mount's horse negotiates an obstacle course alone at the Mounted Police Colloquium at the Kentucky Horse Park. Even though there are other horses present, including barn- and herd-mates, this horse is completely focused on the task at hand. A herd-bound horse is incapable of concentrating on anything other than his best buddy.

Ineffective Riding

Ineffective riding often starts with ineffective riding aids. When a rider gets defensive and goes into the "fetal position," she takes her seat aids off the horse, which also renders her leg aids weak. The horse feels no guidance and is left to his own devices—and to decide what to do next.

Riders' hands, which are developed over time, can present another setback, as discussed in the section about the negative effects of rein tension on p. 68. I recently witnessed a young lady allow her boyfriend, who had no prior riding experience, ride her horse. Though the horse was fairly tolerant of the rank beginner on his back, he trotted off. The girl yelled, "Tighten

ILL-FITTING OR IMPROPER TACK

Tack that doesn't fit properly or is not right for the horse or the horse's job can be a shortcut to ineffective riding. Check your gear each time you ride to ensure you avoid the following:

- A bit sitting too low or loose in the mouth: This not only aggravates the horse, it leaves you without adequate control.
- A saddle too small for you: This leaves you without a good base of control.
- A misused curb bit: The curb is less effective than a snaffle for influencing the horse laterally. It is good for purposes of collection, but falls short, for example, when the horse spins away from something and you try to bring him back. Curb reins may also inhibit impulsion and forward movement.
- Too short stirrups: Unless you are planning to jump during a ride, it is best to have all your aids available, which includes your seat. Short stirrups often take the rider's seat out of the equation. I am sure there are very exceptional hunt seat riders who know how to use their seat with short stirrups, but the average recreational rider can easily lose her seat—and her confidence—with overly short stirrups.

the reins!" which the boyfriend did obediently... but the horse just tucked in his head and went faster. Eventually the horse settled down, but the situation shows how quickly a tense rider with tight reins can escalate a situation from minor to reason for worry.

Other instances of ineffective riding involve the timing concepts I discussed on p. 7, such as failing to correct a horse, or correcting him at the wrong moment. Once, I was giving a riding lesson to a student when all of a sudden, in the middle of it, the horse decided the lesson was over, and headed for the gate. The rider attempted to turn the horse back, but her correction was too late—he had already taken too many steps away from the work area. I tried to allow my student to resolve the difficulty on her own, but the horse kept getting farther away. She did manage to turn his neck, but he just kept heading for the gate with a bent neck. Finally, she brought him back to our workspace, and we returned to the lesson. He pulled the same stunt again. She eventually brought him back again. Then the whole cycle repeated.

It was time for me to intervene. The next time he tried for an early exit, I instructed her to do the following immediately: Reach down for the reins—almost to the bit—and turn the horse decisively in one direction while kicking with her leg on the same side to quickly bring the horse around, spinning him in a very tight circle for several revolutions. We started the lesson again and he tried to head for the gate, but this time she had a ready consequence for his actions. He had pulled that trick for the last time.

Later, the student explained to me that the horse had always pulled that stunt from time to time, but she never knew what to do about it. She had now learned that turning a horse in a tight circle as a consequence for undesired behavior is an extremely effective tool because it puts you in control of his actions. When this horse headed for the gate, he was in control. Spinning him gave control to the rider, and so the horse acquiesced.

One note: Correcting a horse doesn't have to involve cracking him with a crop. I am not opposed to using a crop if necessary, but it is often more productive to have methods of correction handy that don't involve artificial aids.

The Fear Factor

Riders are frightened of their horses for any number of reasons—many of them very legitimate. Perhaps a rider is teamed with "too much horse," or she finds herself on one who has scared her in the past by bolting, rearing, or kicking. Fear is a healthy emotion; it is a natural response we use for survival. But, fear can manifest itself in different ways, and difficulty arises when your fear is such that it paralyzes your response to your horse's actions.

Chesley Sullenberger, the pilot who landed the doomed flight 1549 in the Hudson River in 2009, kept his cool in a terrifying situation. He was able to save more than a hundred lives by keeping his fear at bay as he worked. As Sullenberger did, a rider must maintain some ability to react when presented with a physically threatening circumstance.

"Freezing"

"Freezing" in the saddle while staring blankly ahead is a sure way to get hurt, and I have seen that blank stare many times when teaching new officers to ride patrol horses. One day at work, we were working with a few obstacles, including carrying a flag while mounted. One of the recruits was having serious trouble multi-tasking, as well as reacting when presented with a situation. He would give me the blank stare.

Well, it was a little windy that day, and at one point the recruit's horse quickly moved sideways away from the billowing flag. I had instructed the officers at the beginning to drop the flag and pick up the reins with both hands if they needed to. This recruit didn't do that. Instead, he gripped the reins tighter (we have already discussed the detrimental effects of this reaction—see p. 68) and did so with the flag still in his hand. All the while, I was repeating the words, "Drop the flag. Drop the flag. Drop the flag." But he didn't, and then the flag really annoyed the horse because the recruit pulled it right up close to his head, and finally, the recruit fell off. Fortunately, he was not injured—although his pride suffered a blow.

Not only was his reaction to the scenario wrong, he was not able to listen and carry out instructions at the same time because his fear had "frozen" him. He reverted to what he thought he knew: "Horse goes too fast. Pull back on reins." This makes sense because usually, when we feel physically insecure, we grab more tightly onto whatever happens to be nearby. In the case of reins, however, this is always a very counterproductive maneuver.

Defensive Posture

Another typical reaction to fear is riding in a defensive posture. As I said earlier, a frightened rider tends to get in a "fetal position," collapsing her upper body and bracing in the stirrups with her lower body. Sometimes she purposely tries to keep her legs off the horse, thinking this will prevent bolting, spooking, or jigging. Or, on the other side of the spectrum, she clamps her legs around the horse in a "death grip." Either way, poor riding position puts her in a precarious, top-heavy place, and now not only is the rider afraid—she is also unable to use the aids properly.

How to Confront Fear

Sometimes I see a rider who loves her horse,

A

but is actually afraid to ride him—usually because he is too "hot." Her nervousness in the saddle causes the horse to be apprehensive as well, and everything goes downhill from there. They are fine spending time together during their day-to-day ground activities—grooming, bathing, leading—until it is time to mount up. The fix for this situation involves two steps: The rider needs to improve her skills on an easier, quieter horse, and then take lessons with an instructor on her own. Then both can increase their comfort zones together.

Even the most confident riders face fear at times. When an adult gets hurt, she may lose her confidence, which is very understandable: As we get older, injuries take longer to heal. We can lose time from work and family responsibilities, so a riding injury can have financial impli-

cations as well as physical ones. Facing the potential impact of an injury naturally increases a rider's apprehension and fear every time she gets in the saddle. When this happens, the rider needs to make sure she has a trustworthy horse to help her regain her confidence.

In summary, it is important to have your wits about you so you are able to respond appropriately when you are faced with intimidating moments in the saddle (figs. 4.9 A–C). If the horse or situation scares you so much that you know you will have difficulty reacting, you should dismount, try to deal with the challenge from the ground, or consider a different horse or riding environment. Fear should never paralyze you. If it does, your horse-and-rider team will suffer, and the situation will only worsen.

4.9 A–C   These three riders are handling potentially stressful situations with calm confidence—and their horses are reacting positively to it. Remember, when facing an obstacle or challenge your horse relies on you to keep your seat balanced, your aids clear, and your contact light. Should you sense that you are failing in any of these departments, do not hesitate to dismount and deal with the situation from the ground, as shown by the rider in C.

5

"Compound" Bombproofing Situations

Introduction

Desensitizing your horse to something specific has its obvious uses—clippers, for example—but general bombproofing training has benefits you can apply to *any* situation. Consider one of my most basic bombproofing challenges: walking over a mattress (I provided this lesson in my first book, *Bombproof Your Horse*). People often ask me, "Why should I teach my horse to walk over a mattress? I would never do that in any circumstance." Well, here is why: The more objects you train your horse to walk on or over, the more likely he will readily walk on or through anything you encounter in a real-life situation.

Now, I'm going to take the concept of standard bombproofing training one step further. With a set of all new exercises I call "compound bomproofing"—this means the rider does one thing while the horse deals with something else entirely, and both of you will gain some valuable tools. First, let me give you some classic examples of the kind of situation I'm talking about from the police force. Then I will translate these into civilian application.

Police Work: Multitasking in the Saddle

We mounted police officers often have to do many things at once while in the saddle. Common examples include writing a ticket for an infraction of the law; exchanging paperwork with a driver; talking on a two-way radio; using weapons such as pepper spray, a firearm, or a horse baton; or putting on a gas mask during a disturbance.

THE BATON AND THE DRESSAGE WHIP

I use the Baton Exercise to get a fearful horse used to a dressage whip. I have heard the following statement more times than I can count: "I don't ride with a whip because my horse is afraid of it." This never makes sense to me. If he is afraid of a whip, you need to address the problem, not ignore it. Most horses who fear whips have been abused somewhere along the line, so you need to be patient until he understands that you will not harm him, and explain that the whip is only there to reinforce your leg aids. The horse should *respect* it, not fear it.

The various steps in the Baton Exercise go a long way to improving the whip-shy horse's ability to accept the whip and its proper and fair use.

Other tasks we face daily that the average civilian rider might also deal with include opening a gate; getting the mail; putting on or taking off a coat; carrying something in our hands; picking up or putting down an object; and carrying a flag in a parade.

The training methods for these tasks differ from regular bombproofing sessions because they require multitasking. They also require using just one hand to manage the reins (see p. 58 for details on neck-reining). On the occasion when you need to use *both* hands to accomplish a necessary task, you must take into consideration how best to handle your reins. If you simply drop them on the horse's withers, you risk losing them—for example, when the horse puts his head down to sneak a bite of grass or if he startles, the reins can be jerked so far up his neck you can't reach them. It is best to use long enough reins that in these situations you can loop them over the pommel of the saddle and place them under your knees, which can then hold them in place. Remember, you must leave enough slack in them so you don't create pressure on the horse's mouth. Or, you can slide your arm into the loop of the reins, which allows you to use both hands but still keep the reins under control.

Exercises for the Civilian Rider

The Baton Exercise

I'll start the compound bombproofing with an all-around conditioner for your horse that is similar to the "horse baton drill" we use on the police force. This drill includes physical as well as visual stimuli on both sides of your horse.

To prepare for the baton exercise, buy some inexpensive golf club "protector tubes." Golfers use these to keep their clubs from knocking into each other in their bag. Tubes usually come in black or white. The white ones offer a little more of a challenge because horses can really see them, but either color is fine.

Desensitize on the Ground

Accustom the horse to the tube first by laying it on the ground and asking the horse to approach and examine it. Then, use the tube to stroke the horse, starting at the neck and gradually moving toward his rear. It is best to do this by standing at the horse's near side, with your left hand holding his halter or lead rope while your right hand moves the tube over the horse's body. This way, if the horse tries to scoot or run forward, you can pull him into a circle and let him move around you while you continue with the desensitizing. Eventually, he will realize that you're not trying to harm him, and he will stand still. Your goal is to control his flight response and continue adding the stimulus while the horse assesses the situation. Once you're confident he is accepting the tube on his left side, repeat the process on the right.

Desensitize from the Saddle

Now mount up, and have an assistant on the ground hand you the tube. Hold it in either hand. You should have some semblance of neck-rein influence when you work on this exercise (see p. 58), but if you don't, ride in a round pen. This way, you can stay on a circle and the outside wall will guide your horse.

Hold the tube down at your side and swing it slowly from front to back (fig. 5.1 A). Let the horse dictate how you much and how fast you increase the arc. In other words, if he is running off or getting excited, lower the intensity. Your horse should be under control. As you swing the baton, take some time to pat the horse on the neck and hindquarters. Your goal is to make a complete circle with the baton in your hand.

Once your horse is comfortable with this, start to gradually swing the baton over to the horse's other side, but don't switch hands (figs. 5.1 B & C). Your goal here is to swing it over his head and neck and repeat back and forth. (The motion is similar to what a polo player does with his mallet.) After your horse is desensitized to this action, switch hands, and repeat the same process from the other side.

Once you and your horse are proficient at this exercise, you can get some friends together and play a game of broom polo.

5.1 A-C Alanna swings the golf club protector tube back and forth on Yogi's right side (A). Her goal is to eventually make a complete circle with her arm. Anne demonstrates raising the tube up above Elliott's head, then bringing it over to the opposite side without switching hands (B & C). Her focus is on desensitizing him to the object moving up and over his neck, and behind his head and ears.

The Car Stop

The Car Stop is a basic training exercise designed to acclimate the police horse to make a traffic stop or approach a car in order to speak with the occupant. Don't worry—I am not going to teach you the nuances of law enforcement, but rather give you a training situation that combines schooling the horse with bomb-proofing skills. This is an opportunity for your neck-reining skills to be combined with some of the dressage movements I outlined in chapter 3 (see p. 37).

Phase One

Ultimately, the goal is to be able to approach the car with a driver (and possibly other passengers) inside it, as well as its motor running and the radio blasting. As in other situations, when you begin, you should take the stimulus down to its lowest, so that the car's motor and radio are off, and there is no one in the vehicle. Gradually increase the intensity as you work.

Initially, you may have difficulty getting the horse to move close to the car, so ride him around the vehicle in both directions using the concepts of *comfort zone*, *progression,* and *repetition* that I discuss in chapter 1 (p. 2). If you need extra input, incorporate a *shoulder-in* to help you get closer to the car. Remember, as you circle, the horse's hind end will be pointed toward the vehicle, with his head slightly away. As soon as he will stand near the front car door, ask the driver to give your horse a treat and a pat on the nose (only if the horse likes that sort of thing). After your horse is desensitized to the vehicle, practice schooling exercises nearby: side-pass (p. 58), rein-back (p. 52), turn on the forehand (p. 53), and shoulder-in (p. 49).

Phase Two

Now, in an advanced version of the Car Stop, you will approach the vehicle and exchange items with the driver. A sheet of white paper is a good challenge since it can blow around and make noise. Try a variety of items.

LEANING OVER FROM THE SADDLE

When you have to bend over from the saddle to pick something up, or do the exchange through the car window I describe in Phase Two of the Car Stop—say you're on a tall horse or the car is low to the ground—be mindful of your lower leg on the horse's side next to the car. Riders tend to swing their leg into the horse on the side they are leaning toward (fig. 5.2). This action causes the horse to move away from the leg, and subsequently, the car.

5.2 Jessica demonstrates picking up a low-lying object—here, her dressage whip. Notice how she keeps her left leg off Ringo's side. Bending to the side like this often results in the rider's leg pushing into the horse's side. This signals the horse to move away, and makes picking up the object difficult. Note how Jessica's weight has transferred to her left stirrup. Make sure your girth is secure before attempting this exercise!

The goal is to perform the Car Stop with only one hand on the reins, at all times. You may have to work up to this, however. Using two hands initially is okay, but remember your goal is to progress to one hand—and your weak hand at that—leaving your strong hand available for other tasks (see p. 58 for more on neck-reining). With this in mind, here are the steps to the second phase of the Car Stop exercise (figs. 5.3 A–N):

1 Start parallel to the front of the vehicle and ride around to the driver's side door, giving yourself enough room for a turn on the forehand.
2 Perform a turn on the forehand. Now you're facing the same way as the vehicle and your right side is next to the driver.
3 Side-pass close enough to the car so that the driver can hand you an item such as a clipboard, or a piece or pad of paper.
4 Take the clipboard with your dominant hand (your other hand should be holding the reins), and place it between your saddle and thigh.
5 Rein-back to the rear of the car and then make an "L," so you back around the end of the vehicle. You can stop the exercise here, or if you're up for an additional challenge, go on to Step 6.
6 Write your name and the horse's name on the clipboard or pad of paper. Put it back under your leg.
7 Ride back to the driver's side, but stay about 6 feet away from the side of the car.
8 Side-pass to the vehicle and hand the object back to the driver.

That's it! Repeat the exercise from the passenger's side to work both sides of the horse. Feel free to make up your own variations of the exercise, but bear in mind that the Car Stop

itself is a challenging goal. It is a training situation using something other than a fence, wall, or round pen, with added sensory stimulus from the clipboard and car driver elements.

Opening and Closing a Gate

With this exercise, which is designed for a gate that opens *away* from you, you need to be conscious of your lower leg so that it does not give inadvertent signals to the horse (see sidebar, p. 80). Again, your goal is to do this holding the reins in one hand throughout the exercise (figs. 5.4 A–F).

1 Position your horse parallel to the gate facing the latch (with the hinges to his rear).
2 As you push open the gate, side-pass the horse slightly to follow it, then turn the horse's head into the opening.
3 While still holding the gate, do a turn on the forehand. This should bring you onto the other side of the gate.
4 Side-pass while pushing the gate back to the latching position.

When a gate will only open *toward* you, use the side-pass to get out of the way as you open it. This is more difficult and requires more control. Once you are clear, position your horse's head in the opening, and do a variation of a turn on the forehand—riding forward while the hind end swings around the forehand at the same time. Stop when you are on the other side with the horse's head once again facing the latch end of the gate. Pull the gate back to the closed position and latch it.

Advanced Flag Carrying

A rider carrying a flag can be a big challenge for the horse. First, there is the pole in your right hand (flags are always carried in the right hand) stretching above and behind the horse's head,

5.3 A–N   In the Car Stop, you begin at the front of the vehicle, ride toward the driver's side, making sure to keep enough distance on your left to perform a turn on the forehand (A–C). Ask your horse for a turn on the forehand until you are beside the driver's door (E & F). The driver hands you a piece of paper or a clipboard, which you place under your knee (G & H). Rein-back in an "L" shape around and behind the vehicle (I–K). Write your name on the paper, place it back under your knee, then ride back to driver's side of the car, remaining at least 6 feet away so you can side-pass over to the door, and return the paper to the driver (L–N).

5.4 A–F   Guy and I approach a closed gate, and I use neck-reining to allow my free hand to unlatch and move the gate forward (A & B). Once through the gate, we do a turn on the forehand to face the other direction (C–E), and I side-pass over close enough to shut the gate behind us (F).

5.5 A & B   Anne and Elliot enjoy pole bending with a flag in hand.

where he has a hard time seeing it. Then, there is the flag itself, which always seems to be blowing! *Bombproof Your Horse* offers suggestions for the beginning steps of schooling your horse to carry a flag, so I won't go over that again here. However, I will remind you that you have to neck-rein your horse while carrying out this duty (see p. 58).

When you and your horse are acclimated to the flag—and comfortable carrying it—you can progress to the next level, which is riding with it in various gaits. Practice in a safe enclosure, and don't rush. Practice transitions at a halt, walk, and trot before attempting the canter.

Incorporate patterns into your flag practice. You should be able to ride a figure eight at the walk and trot. One fun and challenging exercise is to ride serpentines through poles or traffic cones (figs. 5.5 A & B).

Firing from Horseback

I discussed acclimating a horse to the sound of gunfire (or a car backfiring) in *Bombproof Your Horse*. In this book, however, I will teach how you desensitize your horse to your shooting a firearm from the saddle. You may wonder why should you do this. One answer is that it gives

you control over the repetition and frequency of a loud noise. If you use firecrackers, for example, you have no control once they start popping. Firing from horseback ratchets the whole process up, presenting a useful challenge for any bombproofing program. A horse that is quiet enough to stand while his rider shoots a gun will tolerate other loud and sudden stimuli, as well. Some other reasons why this exercise may be of value to you:

- You may be interested in "Cowboy Mounted Shooting" (see p. 86, or www.cowboy-mountedshooting.com) and other sports that combine equitation with marksmanship.
- You may hunt or participate in backcountry trips involving hunting from horseback.
- You may be involved in other gun sports and want to combine your hobbies.
- You may ride in an area where you require self-defense (see also chapter 9, p. 137).
- You may participate in historical reenactments.

Firearms to Use

For most of the exercises I've included (I will note exceptions), I recommend that you use a starter pistol, which is not a firearm in the usual

5.6 A starter pistol is appropriate for most of the firing from horseback exercises.

5.7 You can fire blanks out of your regular firearm, although they will expel paper wadding and unexpended powder from the barrel.

5.8 You can purchase plastic cartridge cases and primers to use with your regular firearm, if you own one. These make the gun sound slightly louder than a cap gun but not as loud as a starter pistol or blanks. Simply pop a primer in the designated hole, and after discharging, remove the spent primer and replace it with a fresh one.

sense of the word as it cannot fire projectiles (fig. 5.6). It is used to start races, to sound signals at sporting events, and even for dog training. Most jurisdictions do not treat starter pistols as standard firearms, so they are more readily available. A starter pistol fires .22 caliber blank cartridges that expel only residual powder from the cylinder. There is no functional barrel. If, however, you already own a working firearm, there are ways to incorporate it into your bomb-proofing program. A traditional revolver with

blanks, for example, will desensitize your horse to gunfire just as well as a starter pistol, but do note that blanks for a "real" firearm such as this expel the paper wadding and unexpended powder from the barrel (fig. 5.7). It can also be much louder than a starter pistol, although you can reduce the noise by using a "half load," which means that half of the powder from each blank is removed. Many people who participate in Cowboy Mounted Shooting, a sport in which contestants compete in marksmanship while riding, swear by half loads to prepare for competition. In lieu of a target, riders shoot at balloons that are 10 to 15 feet away from them. The powder and wadding shot out of the firearm's barrel breaks the balloons.

Traditional firearms can even be brought down to a very low noise level by using "primers" only—the little caps used to ignite the rest of the cartridge. Using a primer makes a firearm sound like a "cap gun" (fig. 5.8). Lastly, you can always use a paint ball gun, which is quietest.

Find the pistol and ammunition combination that fits your horse's comfort zone. When your pistol's sound proves too frightening, remove powder from the blank, go to a half load, or use a primer. If you have a starter pistol and it is too loud, you can use a cap gun instead (though bear in mind its firing can be inconsistent). Still too stimulating? Choose the paint ball gun. You can them work progressively back toward the louder firing device.

Before You Begin: The Rules of Handling Firearms on Horseback
Be familiar with your weapon. Ensure your choice of pistol complies with local, county, or state laws. Call your local police to ask what these are. Anyone using a loaded gun should have taken a firearms safety course from local law enforcement or a legitimate community resource. Remember these four main rules:

HOW THEY USED TO DO IT

Back when horses were still used regularly in battle, every cavalry officer had to teach his horse to lie down and to remain so as he was progressively exposed to the noise of gunfire. The cavalry's goal was for officers to be able to fire their weapon from a lying-down position over the top of the horse.

If you get a chance, watch the Clint Eastwood movie *The Outlaw Josey Wales*, and you will see a portrayal of a Confederate cavalry officer who finds himself in an open field while fleeing the Union army. He dismounts and has his horse lie down in the field so they both evade detection. Now *that's* bombproof!

5.9   A US cavalry detachment teaching their horses to lie down in 1900.

1   Treat all firearms as loaded.
2   Never point the muzzle at anything you do not plan to shoot at.
3   Keep your finger off the trigger.
4   Be sure of your target.

In addition, there are issues specific to using firearms while in the saddle, of which you should be aware:

☞ Hold the pistol in your strong (dominant) hand and your reins in your weaker hand. Keep your index finger *off* the trigger and resting on the side of the pistol until you are ready to shoot.

☞ Fire only to the side and never over the horse's head.

☞ If you get into trouble, be ready to drop the gun to the ground. Never attempt to grab the reins with the hand that is holding the pistol.

☞ Any time you need to secure the gun put it in its holster or between your inside thigh and the saddle. Add a lanyard (a cord or strap) if your pistol is fitted to hold one (fig. 5.10). Cavalry officers used lanyards in case they dropped their guns, and mounted police use them today for the same reason.

Dry-Firing

You will begin this exercise by "dry-firing," which means only the clicking sound from the trigger is audible. Ride at the walk with your finger *off* the trigger of an unloaded pistol. Pick a target about 10 feet from you on the ground. (Remember: Never point a gun at something you would not shoot.) Dry-fire (pull the trigger).

If the horse is okay with the first step, then remaining at the walk, bring your arm up to

5.10   When not in use, secure your firearm in a holster. In addition, a lanyard (note the clip and cord attached to the handle of the pistol) prevents accidental drops.

EARPLUGS

Some riders—including mounted shooters, show jumpers, jockeys, and carriage drivers—plug their horses' ears to keep startling noises to a minimum (although not all horses tolerate this). Earplugs will *reduce* noise; they do not eliminate it. Therefore, you can use earplugs during bombproofing if it helps turn the stimulus down enough that your horse can handle it. Don't forget, you *want* your horse to hear some noise—that is the point of bombproofing.

about 45 degrees from your side and slightly behind your leg. Gauge your horse's reaction to this move: Some horses will already have a problem because they do not like your arm being raised. Practice within his *comfort zone* until he grows acclimated so you can move on.

Focus on your target and pull the trigger. You will hear a clicking noise only. Without taking your eyes off the target, assess your horse. Is he fine with what you're doing? If so, lift your arm at a 90-degree angle straight out to the side. Pick another target and dry-fire again. Once your horse is comfortable with your dry-firing at a walk, repeat the steps from a halt (figs. 5.11 A–C).

Live Round
Anytime a gun is loaded with any kind of round—blanks included—we consider it "live." For the next exercise, load a starter pistol or a pistol with blanks and repeat the above proce-

dure with one exception: You will only pull the trigger once. Since this will be a live round (as opposed to the clicking the horse has heard so far), you should expect the horse to react.

Fire the first round pointing at the ground and slightly behind your leg as you practiced before. I recommend this for two reasons. The first is that if the horse is scared, he will likely lurch forward. (When you shoot directly to the side, he is more likely to spin away.) Also, firing behind your leg keeps the noise a little further from his ears.

You must get in the habit of looking at the spot where you shoot. Resist the temptation to look at your horse. Fire a round, and assess the horse's reaction.

You should already have an idea of how he will react from the dry-firing exercise, but if you are nervous about taking this step, add an extra stage for safety: Ask a ground person to fire the gun at your command so you can keep both

5.11 A–C   Anne demonstrates the dry-firing starting position with the gun slightly behind her leg and pointing to the ground (A). She then raises her arm about 45 degrees, to the side but still slightly behind the leg, to keep the sound of the "click" as far away from the horse's ears as possible (B). In the final phase of this exercise, Anne holds the gun straight off to the side and dry-fires again (C).

5.12 A & B   Anne and Elliott jump a small cross-rail while firing at a balloon. This bombproofing exercise is a lot of fun and improves both horse and rider skills.

hands on the reins. Remember your horse does not have to be perfectly still, only manageable.

You should perform both the dry-firing and live round procedures on both sides of the horse. You can "train" by switching hands—that is, switching the hand holding the firearm and the hand holding the reins—but eventually you should learn to fire it using the same hand wherever your target might be. In other words, if right-handed and shooting at a target on the left, you angle your right arm across your body to shoot, leaving the gun in your right hand.

Advanced Training

If your horse and you have the ability to jump at least a small cross-rail (keep in mind you'll be neck-reining on the approach and landing) you might enjoy this challenge. It has the added benefit of being quite fun.

The object is to discharge your pistol while the horse is in flight mode. Since he is airborne, he will be virtually unable to react adversely. In the split second after takeoff, fire the pistol. Pick a target on the ground as usual, or if you're using a pistol with blanks, fasten a balloon to the jump standard to shoot at (figs. 5.12 A & B).

If you and your horse can jump the small cross-rail, but you are a bit hesitant to do it one-handed, have a ground person discharge a round when you are in midflight over the jump. Your horse will learn to deal with the noise at a time when cannot react with a spin or spook, and you may gain the confidence you need to jump and shoot simultaneously.

6

Advanced Trailering Exercises

Introduction

Being able to load your horse in a trailer and transport him is a necessity. Even if you don't show, camp, or otherwise regularly leave the barn with your horse, you may still have to trailer him in a medical emergency. Your goal is to develop the horse's confidence so that he moves forward into the space on his own—at your command.

In my brief discussion of the issue in *Bombproof Your Horse,* I covered a very simple but effective means of teaching your reluctant loader to get into the trailer by using another, experienced horse to lead him in. That is the method we use most for reticent loaders when training new police horses, and it works well because it uses the herd instinct to help a fearful horse realize that the trailer is a safe space.

But, what can you do when a horse still resists, even with another horse calmly entering the trailer first? You can't push the issue in this scenario, because you have a well-behaved horse waiting patiently in the trailer, and taking too long or trying various tricks and techniques may put the willing horse's safety and training in jeopardy. You could wind up with *two* horses that won't load!

So, in the pages that follow, I offer a number of ideas that require a bit more skill on your part using your longeing techniques (see p. 11 for more on longeing). I am not guaranteeing these will fix every trailering dilemma, though. I want to reiterate it is imperative to remember that your technique has to be effective in order to achieve success. A roadblock may be related to *ineffective delivery* of the technique, and not the technique itself. When things aren't working and your horse still will not go in the trailer

GOOD STOCK

A stock trailer is the easiest trailer for loading horses. It is wide open and gives a horse a feeling of "openness" and security. It is probably the best kind to own as your first trailer, since many horses willingly go in one, even if they refuse to enter a straight-load or slant-load. Sure, a stock trailer doesn't offer the creature comforts of a straight-load, but it has distinct advantages for the first-timer.

after you've tried what I outline here, I recommend seeking hands-on professional help from a trainer you trust.

Throughout this chapter, unless I specify otherwise, I am referring to a two-horse, straight-load trailer with a ramp.

Equipment that Helps instead of Hinders

In my opinion, many loading issues begin with the handler trying to lead the reluctant horse into the trailer. When the handler enters the tight space first, the horse typically puts the brakes on at the edge of the trailer ramp.

Trying to address loading issues with special tack and equipment can worsen the situation if you don't know how to use it properly. Even a chain placed correctly over the nose, or a Monty Roberts Dually Halter™—both of which add humane pressure as the horse pulls back and both of which I recommend—won't help you if you apply them incorrectly. You can actually cause more difficulties because the equipment enables you to "force" the horse part

way onto the trailer, and this is when he probably starts pulling back. Guess what happens next? The horse bangs his head on the trailer roof, confirming his fear or creating a new one. Either way, you now have a new problem. Don't get me wrong here; I still recommend using the chain over the nose or the Dually Halter to assist in loading. But, it is imperative you use these tools the right way.

At any point in the loading process, when you have resistance using the trailer simulator setup that I discuss on p. 97, you should immediately put a chain properly over the horse's nose or use a Dually Halter in conjunction with your longe line. If you choose the former, you can either purchase a longe with a chain attached (note: I do not advocate using these for normal longeing purposes—see p. 12), or you can make your own by buying a lead line with a chain, removing the lead fabric or leather, and clipping your longe line to the chain. Run the chain through the metal halter ring under the horse's chin, up through the left side ring, over the horse's nose, and clip it to the opposing link (fig. 6.1). The Dually Halter—my preference, for its ease of use—is simply slipped over the horse's head like any other halter and you snap your longe line to its rings (fig. 6.2). The Dually Halter was created by Monty Roberts, and Roberts explains its proper use in detail in his book *From My Hands to Yours* (www.montyroberts.com). Because it is a piece of specialized equipment, I do recommend familiarizing yourself with Roberts' instructions for the halter's use prior to implementing it.

Whichever device you use needs to teach the horse that *his* actions, not yours, are causing discomfort. As long as the horse goes in the direction you are pointing him, he is free to move as he wishes. The moment he backs away or resists, however, he will experience pressure on the chain or halter across his nose. This ten-

6.1 Here you can see how the chain runs through the metal rings on Elliott's halter and over his nose. It is clipped to the side ring on the right side.

6.2 A Dually Halter fitted over Elliott's bridle.

sion is relieved when he moves forward again. Practice this very basic application and release of pressure without asking anything of the horse other than that he comes to you. Stand in front of him and apply pressure on the halter until he moves toward you. As soon as he takes a step, relieve the pressure and pat him. Repeat the exercise several times.

When the horse understands that he is in control of releasing the pressure by moving forward, ask him to back up at your request (you'll need to be able to back your horse out of the trailer, so best to practice a little now). Standing on the horse's left, turn and face his tail, apply light pressure on the longe line, and take a step toward his hind end. Ask him to "Back." Again,

it is up to the horse to find the correct response to your request in order to make the pressure on his nose cease. When he takes a backward step, release the pressure and praise him.

The Case for Giving Treats

Before I get into specific ways of approaching trailering difficulties, I want to address the use of treats when training your horse. Rewarding animals with food they like is one way to elicit a desired response from an animal. (Well, not all animals. Cats will respond only when they feel like it.) I do not disparage using treats, but they have never offered me a practical solution. (I can't carry around bags of horse treats while I am riding on patrol.) That being said, trailer loading lends itself well to their use for positive reinforcement. After all, horses eat in the trailer, so most already associate it with food. There are plenty of times that horses have been persuaded to walk into a new or dark trailer simply by showing them a bucket of feed. If that's all it takes and it works, by all means do it. You don't need to be a horse whisperer to do that.

In the case of a slightly more reticent horse, I think it is fine to reward him every time he takes even one step a little closer to the trailer, or a little further in. However, make sure you are using proper reward techniques—that is, only reward your horse for a *positive* response; don't bribe him. Another food-related trick that I find works is to regularly load the trailer-shy horse at feeding time for a week or so, and let him eat his breakfast or dinner in the trailer. He should fast become well acclimated and hop right in the next time you need to go somewhere.

Do use "healthy" treats where possible, such as cut-up carrots and apples, or commercially prepared but nutritious ones. Junk food isn't any better for horses than it is for humans.

6.3 A–C I longe Elliott with a regular halter and longe line (no chain) into and through this confined space meant to simulate the feel of a horse trailer. Because he longes well and obediently, he quickly grows accustomed to the strange obstacle.

Problem "Loaders"

The techniques I am going to present now are a bit more complex. They are best suited for those horses that do not respond either to proper equipment and handling technique, food and treats, or the "herd instinct" method mentioned earlier and detailed in *Bombproof Your Horse*. In these cases, you need to consider where the horse's reluctance to load is coming from. Has the horse had a bad experience in the trailer? Does he need extra understanding and patience? Or, is he just plain being obstinate? Maybe he doesn't want to load—which he assumes means go to work—because his buddies are out playing in the field.

Your approach must consider the horse's motivation (or lack thereof). For example, if your horse had an incident in a trailer at any point in his life, you may have a real challenge on your hands. You might be able to get the horse to go up the ramp or put one foot in the trailer. And, it may take an hour just to do that. As long as you have progressed a little bit, you can praise and reward him, and let it go until the next trailer loading session. For any horse-training issue, repetition, as I've said before, is part of the solution, and trailer loading is no exception. You can't work with the horse once a month and expect him to improve. You have to spend time working on the problem area at least every other day.

To establish the root of the loading problem, let's begin by looking at your horse's ability to move forward on the longe line at your request. (See instruction on the different types and applications of longeing on p. 11.) If your horse is attentive to you, will move forward at the various gaits and halt on your command, then you are ready to proceed.

Back to Basics: The Confined Space
Once your horse longes obediently, you can

set up a simulated trailer or trailering situation and longe your horse into the confined space (figs. 6.3 A–C). Do this by hanging a tarp on the arena fence or securing a solid piece of plywood next to it. About 4 feet away from the fence toward the inside of the arena, set up a second tarp (or another piece of plywood) supported by a horizontal pole on short jump standards, barrels, or cinder blocks. If you use tarps, secure their corners so they don't blow around. (Note: I find that using tarps is better than solid plywood, because they cannot physically harm the horse.) As you longe your horse into and through the simulated trailer setup, you need to make sure that the longe line doesn't get caught on the "inside wall." Leaning a ground pole at an angle on either end often helps the longe line slide up and over the "wall," or you can simply make the inside wall quite low so it isn't an issue.

Advancing the Simulated Trailer Exercise

When your horse is comfortable moving through the confined space, ask him to halt on the longe line when he is positioned between the "outer" and "inner walls." Pause for a moment, then go ahead and send him all the way through. Repeat.

When he does this easily and calmly, increase the intensity. Place a barrier in front—a raised ground pole or cavalletti will work—or move your simulated trailer to the corner of the arena where the arena fence or wall can form the front barrier. Send the horse in as far as he will go, maintaining a light contact on the longe line (figs. 6.4 A–D). Let him stand for a moment, then either approach him and back him out with light tension on the longe line, or ask an assistant to help guide him out of the simulator.

This simulation setup isn't perfect because it doesn't have a roof and it is limited by the

height of the fence in the arena. So, if you are really ambitious, build your simulator using PVC pipe and tarps. This way you can extend the height of the side walls, include a "roof," and even use a sheet of very heavy-weight plywood as a mock ramp.

Showtime

Once your horse willingly enters and stands within the three-sided simulator, it is time to try using the trailer itself. Set your horse up for success by parking *inside* a riding arena, paddock, or pasture with the trailer's right side as close to a fence or wall as possible (fig. 6.5). You want to eliminate any possibility of the horse running out on that side. The fence, in this case, is your inanimate assistant. And because you are in an enclosed space, you don't have to worry if your horse gets away from you at any point in the process.

When using a two-horse trailer with a ramp, either remove the middle partition or slide it over to one side so the horse has plenty of room, and open the side escape doors to give a comforting feeling of "openness." (Make sure the chest bars are secured.) When using a stock trailer, however, leave the "people door" shut—you don't want the horse to attempt to exit through it. I've

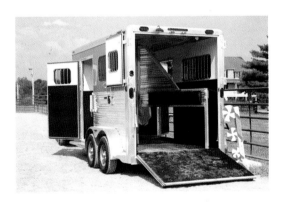

6.4 A–D   I send Elliott into the simulator using the Dually Halter and longe line (see p. 94). This time he can't go all the way through, because I've set it up in the corner of the arena. This particular day present- ed a challenge because it was very windy and the tarps were blowing. But, Elliott managed to overcome any hesitation and enter the space as I asked because his work on the longe line and in-hand is well con- firmed. Note my use of the longe whip as a quiet, but additional, cue to go forward.

6.5   This two-horse, straight-load trailer with a ramp is properly set up for the loading exercise. Both side doors are open, the chest bars are secured, and the partition is pulled to the side, creating an "open" environment for the horse. The trailer is parked as close to the fence as pos- sible, which prevents the horse from running out to the right side. In this case, we also added the pink and white jump standards to fill a gap with an additional "inanimate assistant."

seen it happen! Enlist the help of an assistant so you have human help if you need it.

Now, send the horse into the trailer just as you did during the simulated exercise. If you did your homework, he should respond to your requests willingly. Be persistent in getting him to focus his attention on the trailer. Any attempt to run away from the trailer should result in resis- tance from the nose chain or Dually Halter. If he runs off to the left side where you are probably

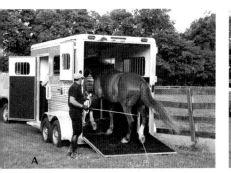
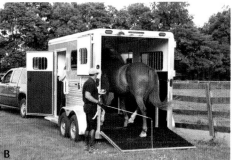

6.6 A–C   I longe Elliott onto the trailer, with the help of an assistant up front who rewards him with treats when he takes a step further inside. Note my steady contact on the longe line and how I hold the longe whip behind Elliott to "test" and see if he'll go a little further in. I lower it when he's all the way on.

standing (since the right side is blocked by the fence) be prepared to flick the longe line or longe whip to keep him from running you over.

Troubleshooting Trailer Loading

When the horse still refuses to enter the trailer, put him immediately into a small circle around you near the back of the trailer. Longe him at the trot for a few minutes, then send him forward toward the trailer again. As soon as you get him to put his front feet on the ramp, praise him profusely and have an assistant give him a treat. If he steps off again, put him back in the longe circle. This way he earns that the trailer is good (he can rest and receive praise) and that evading it means he has to go to work.

Do not continue to feed the horse after his first small treat for taking a step up the ramp. From here on out, he needs to give you *more* cooperation before he gets more reward. If the horse is now standing quietly on the ramp of the trailer, don't try to force him further in. Instead, ask him to back up (see p. 95) and lead him away from the trailer. Remember: *You* are asking him to step away from the ramp. It wasn't his idea. Give him a little break.

Now, longe the horse toward the trailer again at whatever gait he likes. Of course, you don't want him running into the trailer, but a quiet trot in is all right (walking, of course, is preferable). Repeat the above process until he goes further in than he was before. Keep a light and steady contact with the longe line, because it if is too loose, he will step on it or get tangled. And, if it is too tight, his forward movement will be hindered. If he decides at any point to leave the trailer on his own, put him to work and send him immediately back in. Do not praise him or give him a break when it is his idea to back out—only when it is yours.

You can test the horse after several repetitions of the steps above by raising the longe whip behind him to see if he will go a little further in with your urging (6.6 A–C). This entire process needs to be repeated daily, if possible, until the horse comfortably walks into the trailer by himself (6.7 A–H). Once this happens, put the partition back in place to advance the exercise, and repeat the loading scenario several more times to confirm it.

In Case of Emergencies

As I mentioned in the beginning of this chapter,

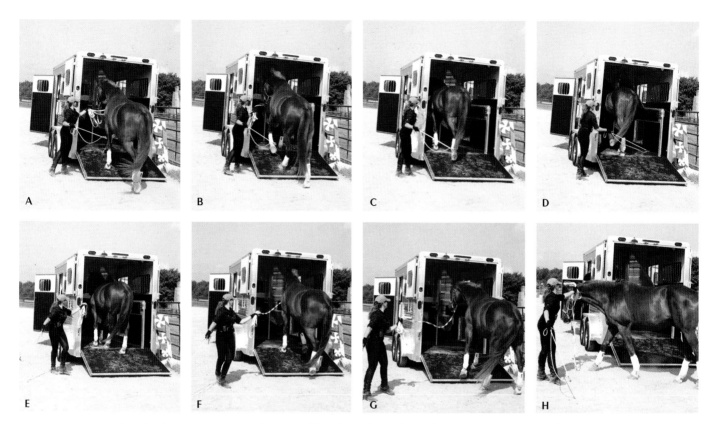

6.7 A–H Anne demonstrates longeing Elliott into the trailer without an assistant. Notice that as Elliott makes his way up the ramp, enters, and then stands quietly inside, Anne keeps a light contact with the longe line—she gives him enough room to move forward on his own, but doesn't let the line dangle dangerously (A–C). She uses the longe whip to indirectly encourage Elliott to continue forward and bring his last foot off the ramp and into the trailer (D). After a minute or two in the trailer, Anne signals for Elliott to back out, pointing the whip away and maintaining her contact on the line (E–G). He turns and comes to Anne for praise and a pat (H).

you can always load a quiet, experienced horse in the trailer with the reluctant one to help ease the trailer-shy horse's mind. But let's say you absolutely *must* get the horse into the trailer right now—due to an emergency of some kind—and putting a calm horse in first isn't working or isn't possible. Well, if you have ever watched racehorses enter the starting gate, you have probably seen a horse that is being difficult loaded by professionals. One person leads the horse, while two

others lock forearms around the horse's hind end just above the hocks, and they basically shove the horse in and quickly close the gate behind him.

Don't worry. I am *not* advocating that you try this technique with your own reluctant loader. Leave that to the professionals at the racetrack. However, there is one method—a variation of the starting-gate technique—that you should be able to employ if an emergency arises and loading your horse is necessary.

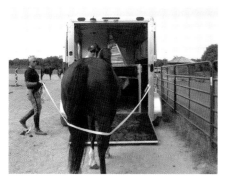

6.8 If your horse remains a difficult loader, even though you've worked to acclimate him to the trailer, using a longe line and extra handler is an appropriate back-up plan to use *in case of emergencies only.* When I say "emergency," I mean your horse must get on the trailer *right now.* In all other cases, I believe you should work through his fears gradually as I've outlined. The longe line method puts pressure on the horse's hind end to encourage him forward. You need a handler at the horse's head to guide him into the trailer.

Instead of locking arms with another handler, you can use a rope or strong longe line around the horse's hind end to encourage him to move forward (fig. 6.8). This technique is the exception to my rule about not having a person lead the horse into the trailer. In this case, you need another handler at the horse's head. Her job is to guide—not force—the horse into the trailer. She should not pull or apply too tight contact or she risks the horse pulling back and striking his head on the roof of the trailer. All pressure must come from behind. Here are some tips for making this method work when necessary:

- Have one handler on each side of the horse and another at his head. The horse will often attempt to evade to one side or the other. The two rear handlers stretch the longe line or rope between them and bring it up against the horse's hind end, just above his hocks where they apply steady pressure.
- If you can only find one extra ground person to help, take one "escape route" out of the equation by parking the trailer with its right side close to a wall or fence.
- Again, if you only have a handler to help at his head, you can securely tie the right side

of the longe line or lead rope to the trailer or fence. You then operate the line from the left side, applying pressure to the hind end (just above the hocks) to encourage the horse to step into the trailer.
- The handler at the horse's head is there for slight corrections—keeping the horse centered and disallowing him from turning off the ramp. She is *not* there to pull, just to guide.
- An alternative position for a third handler is near the horse's hindquarters with the longe whip. This is only applicable if the horse usually responds well to a flick of the whip and displays no fear of it. You should *never* crack the whip aggressively, or strike the horse with it

Self-Loading

Why should you even bother to teach a horse to walk on a trailer by himself? Well, have you ever been alone, walked your horse onto the trailer, then ran around to the back to secure the "butt bar' before he backed out? Has the horse ever tried to back out again before you could get there and stop him? To avoid getting myself into these situations, I have trained every horse I have ever had to walk onto the trailer by himself. For me, it is a must.

Here is a very simple solution that I use on the rare occasion when I'm loading by myself and my normally cooperative horse doesn't self-load immediately. (Even police horses have a mind of their own.) I position myself on the horse's *off* (right) side and lead him onto the trailer, and I walk into the empty stall on the right while he walks into his stall on the left (fig. 6.9). This way, I have worked within his comfort zone while making sure I'm in position to fasten up the "butt bar" in a safe and timely manner.

Even though I have this option at the ready, I still prefer my horses self-load. It isn't hard to teach this lesson once you've acclimated your horse to the trailer in general.

6.9   Anne loads Elliott from the offside. This is a better option when you are alone and need to lead your horse into the trailer as it allows you to fasten the "butt bar" in a safe and timely manner.

The Buddy System

Let's assume your horse willingly walks on the trailer—that is, as long as you walk in with him. It doesn't have to be this way, since it is very easy to teach the horse to load himself. You can use the "herd instinct technique" described in

Bombproof Your Horse because most horses will willingly walk into a trailer on their own when they see another horse in there. So, first condition your horse to load on his own with the other horse. When you start the process, load the other horse first, then the horse you're teaching to self-load. Then, in order to gradually wean your horse away from his buddy, try having him self-load first, immediately followed by loading his buddy up beside him. Finally, extend the amount of time your horse is in the trailer without his buddy. This method works the vast majority of time with new police horses. But, to be candid, at the police training facility, we have the luxury of training trailer loading 40 hours a week if we need to, and can load horses in and out of the trailer several times a day. You may not have that kind of flexibility.

TRAILERING TACK

Mounted police officers are in and out of the trailer too much to wrap their horses up like Christmas packages in head bumpers, shipping boots, and so on. Thus, it is common practice to transport police horses for patrol already tacked up (minus the bridle). Sometimes, for tactical reasons, we have to keep all tack and riot gear on the horses in order to respond quickly to a problem area. Meanwhile, the horses are taught to stand quietly in the trailer, fully suited up.

Horse on Board—Now What?

Closing the Ramp or Rear Door

Before you actually go for a test drive, you need

to shut the trailer's back door, which can be difficult with a horse that is reluctant to load in the first place. After you've loaded him, fasten the "butt bar," and *immediately* shut the rear door or ramp. In fact, it is a good idea to have two people, one on each side of the door or ramp, to make sure it is closed quickly. When you are using a stock trailer, note that the hinged doors take longer to close, so you have to act the instant you get the horse inside. After all the work you've put into persuading your reluctant loader on board, you don't want him to back into the bar, kick at it, or break through and scare himself.

Driving with Caution

The next step is to set the trailer in motion with your trailer-shy horse on board. Use care: Stay on the farm or on nearby roads so you can return quickly if necessary, or take help with you in the truck.

Now that your horse is in the trailer, you may need to alter—or at least be more conscientious about—your driving habits. Bad driving can mess a horse up forever. I have seen horses become reluctant loaders and, even worse, difficult cargo because of bad driving. Driving a horse trailer is not like driving a normal car. Stopping distance is greater. Cornering needs to be done more slowly. Acceleration must be smooth and consistent.

When you toss your horse about in a straight-load trailer, what do you think happens? He will either decide he is never getting in a trailer again, or he'll get on but throw himself against the side of the trailer to brace himself in anticipation of the upcoming ride. He'll take a "life-preserving" posture to protect himself. Most "leaners" pick one side to brace on: A horse that decides left will always lean against the left side; those that go right lean against the center partition (unless you always load them

into the right stall). The problem with the habitual lean is that it's possible for a horse to fall if he's leaning the wrong way through a turn.

Unfortunately, you can't send the horse to a therapist to discuss what's upsetting him, or use logic to convince him that leaning actually makes things worse. The best solution I have found is to put your leaning horse in either a slant load or a stock trailer, or pull the partition in your straight-load out. Now your horse can have the whole trailer to himself. With the extra room, he can spread his legs as much as possible, and will naturally stand at a 45-degree angle if left to his own devices. (This is actually a strong argument for only using slant-load trailers, although I still prefer the regular straight-loads.) With much time and patience, the horse may be able to transition back to "normal" trailering practices.

Persistence, Understanding, and Time

In summary, remember that you have a lot of options when teaching a reluctant loader to accept the trailer. You need to be more persistent than the horse, and you also need to understand the cause of his refusal to load and take it into consideration as you decide which methods to use in retraining.

Respect the time factor. To teach a reluctant loader to get into a trailer peacefully, you will need to be willing to spend the time necessary and not cut corners. Do not let too many days pass between training sessions or you will have to start over from square one. Be consistent, patient and use *progression*, *repetition*, and proper *reward and punishment* techniques (see chapter 1, p. 3).

7

Becoming a Parade Pro

Introduction

My first book, *Bombproof Your Horse,* included some preliminary suggestions for riding in parades. This time, I'm delving deeper into both logistics and safety considerations for those who plan to participate in such performances. Whether you are riding in a small-town Fourth of July celebration or a national event, the concerns are mainly the same.

Preparing for the Parade

Exposure
Before you take a horse to a big parade, try a small local event first (fig. 7.1). How he performs in this atmosphere will give you an idea if he has what it takes to be a good parade mount. You're not asking him to be perfect, just manageable.

Shoeing
Since asphalt is not the ideal surface for a shod horse to walk on, you may need to alter your horse's shoes. It can help to add a traction device, such as borium (a trade name for the mineral tungsten carbide), or Drill-Tek (tungsten carbide particles set in a brass/silver solder matrix), or some other substance (fig. 7.2). It might be easiest to have your farrier shoe with borium nails, which are regular nails with tungsten carbide dabbed on their surface. You can also have your horse go barefoot. Unshod hooves provide great natural traction, and if you're only participating in one parade, you won't be riding on pavement long enough to wear them down.

7.1 Riders in a small-town parade. It is a good idea to test your horse in small, local event before trying one on a grander scale.

7.3 Police units are generally on the clock when in parades. Here, two young police mounts are being "street trained" in a local parade.

7.2 When planning to ride in a parade, you need to consider your horse's footwear—asphalt can be slippery under the standard shoe. There are several kinds of traction devices and/or substances that can be added to your horse's shoes to help keep him on his feet. Here, the red arrows point to the studs added to the heels of this shoe.

Sometimes, you may not have a choice—for example, the Inaugural Parade in Washington, DC, requires every horse wear shoes treated with borium. When parade organizers stipulate a certain type of shoeing, you have to obey if you want to participate.

Organize Your Group

When you establish a group of riders for a parade, choose a leader and a second in command. It is important that in a stressful situation one person is in charge; this avoids too many riders weighing in. A leader has to make decisions based upon the information on hand at the time in question. You can't take a vote on everything, so choose a leader who can keep her cool and make an informed decision.

Dealing with Those in Charge and Addressing Special Considerations

Always assume that parade organizers know *nothing* about horses. They may think they have horse experience because of their involvement in previous parades, but they'll certainly know little about your horse and his particular needs. Do not be afraid to bring issues up and negotiate: Try to overcome organizational concerns by offering a solution. For example, parade organizers often want to put horses at the end of the parade so other participants don't step in manure. To alleviate this worry, offer to provide someone to follow the horses and provide clean-up. This individual can be in a pick-up truck (you can decorate it to make it part of the parade) or on foot with a muck bucket on wheels. It's good public relations. As a mounted police unit, we usually go up near the beginning of the parade with the other police honor and color guards. This is for budgetary reasons: Police units are on the clock, so we need to play our part in the parade and then resume other work-related duties (fig. 7.3).

Although civilian groups don't usually have the same time constraints, you will face many of the same challenges that police units do. For example, there could be road construction along the route, involving sections of the street covered with steel plates, which are way too slippery and dangerous for horses. Parade organizers won't recognize this as an issue. You will need to familiarize yourself with the parade route and plan how to negotiate questionable road conditions (see more about this on p. 108). Get a map showing the streets parallel so you know how to access the staging area and exit when finished, since the actual route will be closed to traffic. Ask the organizers about the return access route to parking. Will it be open to you the whole time, or closed until the parade is over?

Find out your estimated "step-off" time. If the parade begins at 10:00 AM, you will likely be told to stage at 9:00 AM, but if your position is toward the end of the parade, you may not step off until noon or later. This means standing around for three hours—a kind of prolonged waiting that can cause boredom and agitation in any horse—so, if you can, it's good to base your arrival on step-off time rather than staging assignments

TIPS FOR PARADE ORGANIZERS

If you have the opportunity to discuss the parade with its organizers, offer them some of the tips I've outlined below so they can better accommodate horse units without taking a complete course in horsemanship.

- Horse units should have their own parking area so they are not around loud and raucous marchers, such as bands. The less public access to this area, the better.
- If parking is positioned at the end of the parade route, riders require an access route to the staging area.
- If parking is positioned at the beginning of the parade route, riders require a return access route from the end.
- Do not put horse units between—or specifically, in front of—marching bands, cheerleaders, fire engines, or Shriners in their little cars. Put horse units between "quiet" groups, such as scouts or politicians.
- Water troughs should be easily accessible away from crowds of people. Horses shouldn't have to negotiate "chaos" to get to water.
- For very large parades, like the Rose Bowl or Inaugural, with lots of horse units, there should be a farrier and veterinarian on scene.
- Establish emergency access routes in advance since many roads are closed during the parade.

7.4 This group of horses parades down a very narrow street. They haven't much room to walk abreast and leave room near the curb for onlookers. A wide street is far preferable for horse units.

Get a lineup of participants as soon as possible to find out who is parading directly in front and behind your group. When you will have a marching band, twirling dancers, or people shaking large balloons near you, you need to prepare yourself.

"Recon" the Route

"Recon" the area! To "recon" is a military and police term, which means to "scout." If you are not familiar with the parade route, I strongly suggest you assure yourself that conditions are adequate.

I have often ridden in the Fourth of July parade in Takoma Park, Maryland, which is very challenging. Its roads are sometimes wide and sometimes narrow. The approach to the reviewing stand is on a narrow residential street that is mostly downhill. People are crowded right to the sidewalk's edge, with many sitting on the curb. Four horses abreast is the safe maximum, giving you a little buffer in case a horse shies to the side (fig. 7.4).

Because of the narrow streets and the crowd being so close to the horses, I often say that the Takoma Park Parade is, in fact, far more challeng-

ing to the horse than the St. Patrick's or Cherry Blossom Parades on Constitution Avenue, a main boulevard in Washington, DC. Constitution Avenue, although grander and more intimidating, is actually safer—a wide street has a huge *comfort zone* between horses and onlookers.

In addition to checking out parking availability (see below), reviewing the staging area is a key part of your recon work. Some parades, like the Inaugural, are very strict. In these cases, you are given a very specific (and often inadequate) area in which to get ready.

Parking and Truck Logistics

Consider carefully where to park your truck and trailer—ahead of time, if you have a choice in this matter. Organizers, who may or may not be considerate of the needs of horses, often provide parking near the start, which means you have to ride all the way back (probably via an alternate route, see p. 107) after the parade is over. I prefer to park at the end of the route. This way, you can quickly load up and leave. Another benefit: the horses get warmed up as you ride to the staging area (see p. 110).

Some people prefer to park nearer the staging area. It gives you access to your hay and water while you are waiting, and being close to your trailers allows the group to rest more comfortably until you have to get in line.

If you can arrange your own parking, consider shopping center parking lots (get permission first) or public parking lots bearing in mind these can get very full during a parade and you may get blocked in. (I discussed this at some length in *Bombproof Your Horse*.) In all cases, parking near a flat grassy area—with room to ride and calm a nervous animal—is ideal (figs. 7.5 A & B).

If possible, arrange to have a spare set of keys to the truck and trailer you came in. This way, if something unforeseen happens and the

7.5 A & B   A horse unit prepares for their ride in the parking area. This includes grooming, tacking up, readying flags and props, and keeping the horses comfortable and calm.

driver has to leave the parade, you can get into the vehicles and you won't be stranded. If you don't have spare keys, you should stick with the person who drove you there, and if you take a break, take it together.

Extra Vehicle

A "runaround vehicle," otherwise known as a spare car or truck, is another helpful extra. Should you suddenly need a piece of equipment, like a rein or stirrup leather, the person assigned to the spare car can bring it to you easily without having to disconnect the truck and trailer. Give the driver the map of parallel streets that I mentioned earlier (see p. 107).

You may even put the runaround vehicle in the parade if allowed. If you have promised the organizers manure pickup, it can serve this purpose. And, it has yet another benefit: Your vehicle can serve to create a buffer between you and the group marching behind you—especially helpful if it is a noisy marching band.

Extra People

Plan carefully for your personnel needs. When you're attending a small parade you may not need anyone other than the participants. However, in addition to the helpful volunteer who has agreed to deal with the manure, and the individual to drive the runaround vehicle, you may want to assign someone to stay with the trailers, so should one be needed it can be brought to you during the parade. This person also prevents your trailers from being blocked in by others.

Also consider drafting another generous person to walk beside or behind you (when needed as a buffer) during the parade. This is a particularly useful idea when you have a new horse likely to spook. The "walker" should have some horse experience and at least one halter and lead rope with her at all times, and preferably should not have any other responsibilities so she is free to help in case of an emergency. She can also carry the "emergency" pack of information I discuss on p. 110.

Extra "Stuff"

Bring all you need—including feed, hay, and water—so you are self-sufficient. Your average parade does not have many horses in it, so you should assume organizers have not provided water. We fill

7.6 A & B The staging area can be a loud, raucous scene—do your best to steer your horse clear of the crowds and floats, and try to keep his mind and body busy and distracted (A). As your step off time nears, stand in simple formation facing the same direction (B).

the big plastic jugs that go in office water coolers. Figure that you need to bring about one 10-gallon jug for each horse on a hot day.

Pack an extra rein, girth, stirrup leather, lead rope, and halter, and extra clothing like rain gear. You also should have a bag loaded with equipment, such as duct tape, safety pins, injectable Acepromazine, a first aid kit, an extra lead rope, and a leather punch for tack repair. Have a member of your helpful support team bring this along during the parade.

Mobile phones are great when they work, but when cell service is a concern, consider arming your group with walkie-talkies. They have a limited range and open airwaves so strangers may be on your frequency, but they are a handy way for the leader to communicate with the trailer "sitter" or driver of the runaround vehicle.

Documents and Paperwork
All too often, paperwork is an afterthought. It is crucial, however, to collect all the information that the parade organizers have provided. It may contain the lineup and a confirmation note

proving that you were invited. These documents are vital when the officials on site are missing your listing, or have moved your starting position at the last minute without consulting you.

Bring along emergency contact forms and permission slips for underage riders. And, as you should always do when riding away from home, carry any pertinent horse and human health information—copies of Coggins tests, medication requirements, lists of food or pharmaceutical allergies—in case there is an emergency.

Your group leader should carry one copy of all the paperwork with her in the parade, and another member of the group should have another. This way, should the leader somehow become separated from the group, you have a backup person with important documents.

Parade Day

Staging Area
On the day of the parade, always ride in formation even when not on the official parade route.

Keep your group riding in pairs, at a minimum—it looks much more professional. Ride in formation from your parking area to your assigned staging area. When you arrive, do your best to keep clear of any distractions, such as bands or clowns. The staging area can be full of strange and "scary" costumes, sounds, and floats.

The person with the quietest horse and one buddy, or your ground helper, should check in with a parade marshal. Ask him to point out which group you follow so your group will be ready when it is your turn.

As it nears time for your group to step off, stand in a formation such as a simple line so you are all facing the same direction (figs. 7.6 A & B). Position the horses so their hind end is least likely to be approached by a spectator. Line up in front of objects such as trees or structures. When your group is in disarray, the risk of a human getting kicked when one horse decides to let another horse "have it" increases.

Settling the Horse Down

This should go without saying, but *do not* rely on Acepromazine or any other horse tranquilizer to get you through a parade. It is *never* a good idea. Some horses actually behave worse: Reaction to such a drug is unpredictable and a horse may be rendered unsafe to ride. Better to use the schooling techniques I outlined on p. 37 to calm your horse beforehand. A well-schooled horse will quiet down when you find a flat area to work him, such as a playing field or park. Just do your best to get him settled *before* you proceed to the staging area.

Safety Tips

Even when riding in a parade, you should wear a helmet. I know there are times that dictate otherwise—such as when you are riding in period costume. The mounted police have a dress uniform with a soft hat, for example.

However, helmets really are the safest way to go, so when you can work around your garb somehow, wear one.

Never ride off and leave a fellow rider alone. For those who think that every horse person should know better than to do this, watch how often it happens. Many accidents have occurred because of inconsiderate riders. Even a good horse gets upset when he sees his "herd" leaving him.

It is even worse when that lone rider is still trying to adjust tack or equipment, or mount up. The latter is always a dangerous moment—as is dismounting. As my friend Sergeant Mayo from the Royal Canadian Mounted Police (more commonly known as the "Mounties") says, "When you mount up, *mount up*." The sooner you are in the saddle, the safer you are (figs. 7.7 A & B).

Check your girth when you get on and again after riding for a while. It doesn't hurt to periodically check it throughout the day. This is one of those things I don't do enough. Yes, even I get complacent sometimes!

Troubleshooting Common Scenarios

When you encounter a setback in the parade, be prepared to act. Of course, I can't possibly cover every eventuality, but here are some general issues I have dealt with before.

1   Have an "exit" planned when a horse cannot settle down and is becoming unmanageable. You may have to pull an uncontrollable horse from the parade detail. But, remember, you should never send one horse and rider off alone. Another horse—preferably a calm one—should go along to provide a source of sensible support. You will need to decide if it is best to ride the horse away, or dismount and lead him. Choose your exit route carefully. Of course, if you have arranged for someone to walk with the group in case of just such an emergency,

7.7 A & B It is important to get in the saddle as quickly and smoothly as possible (A). Mounting and dismounting put the rider at a disadvantage as her balance and stability is compromised. And, in a parade situation, it is likely that your horse will be anxious and need to move forward right away (B), so be prepared to put him to work with a little schooling exercise (see p. 37).

she can help with the horse and provide a halter and lead rope, if necessary.

2   Let your horse look at what's following him in the parade.
It may seem odd, but I have found it best to simply turn a frightened horse around to face the float or band that's scaring him during a pause in the parade's forward movement. This way he can see what is worrying him. Frequently, once a horse can look at whatever is causing the strange noises, he will settle down.

I had an officer in Washington, DC's Cherry Blossom Parade who refused to let his horse turn around. Guess what? The horse flipped over attempting to do just that. (So much for borium. He slipped anyway.) The officer hit his head, but he was all right, and fortunately, we had a ground person with us that day who helped remove the horse from the parade.

3   Be alert at all times to potentially dangerous situations.
Many riders are guilty of becoming complacent, especially after you've ridden in a couple of parades. When you see kids running toward you with flying balloons, tell them—or their parents—to stop and secure the balloons. Maybe your horse doesn't mind them, but the others may. It's better to be safe than sorry, as the cliché goes.

4   Plan your formation according to your group's horses' temperaments.
Other distractions that crop up beside you along the parade route are umbrellas, baby strollers, wheelchairs, dogs, flags, and the wind blowing all that stuff around (fig. 7.8). Balloon vendors and clowns are sometimes difficult, but the main problem is spectators right on top of you, particularly on a narrow road. So, place your strongest, calmest horses on the outside of your formation. Since the leader of a parade

7.8 Inspector Moses Cortwright in the police parade, New York City. Although on a nice wide road, you can see the kinds of flags, people, and general fanfare horses have to deal with in these situations.

group always rides on the far right (see p. 114), he needs to have a good, solid horse. Always assume that the public does not understand a horse's nature.

5   Be ready to deal with a rider fall.
When an incident occurs and a rider falls off, the parade is held up. Keep firmly in mind that horse and rider safety is more important than the parade staying on schedule. If your group is being rushed, or a situation occurs that requires your group to stop, wait until it is fully resolved before moving on.

Treat the incident as the fire department and police treat any traffic accident—that is, "secure the scene." In civilian language, this means keep people away from the victim. The parade simply cannot go around when you have an injured horse or rider on the street,

and as inconvenient as it may be for others in the parade and onlookers, the parade can wait. People coming and going can cause injuries, especially when you are trying to calm a frightened horse. There should be parade officials along the route to help you. Send someone to alert an official if an incident occurs.

Communication and Formation

Hand Signals
Hand signals are invaluable for mounted police during crowd control because usually there is so much noise the riders often cannot hear each other. They are also useful for large groups during a parade.

The War Department Field Manual FM 2-5, Cavalry Drill Regulations, Horse (March 13, 1944)

7.9 Here are some of the hand signals from the War Department Field Manual FM 2-5, Cavalry Drill Regulations, Horse (March 13, 1944). I've included the ones most appropriate for use in a parade, or riding in formation in general.

provides hand signals and commands for just this sort of situation (fig. 7.9). If you were to read the entire cavalry manual, you would probably be overwhelmed. I doubt that any civilian group planning to ride in a parade has enough horses to constitute a "company," as groups are called in the cavalry, so I will stick to keeping things simple for you and assume you are riding with a dozen or fewer horses. In cavalry terms, you will be riding as a "section."

The simplest formation is to ride next to each other as long as you can all fit across the street comfortably without coming too close to the curbs. On residential streets, for example, this will probably mean riding four abreast (see p. 116).

"Dress"

The wider the line, the harder it is to maintain "dress," which is the concept of keeping the horses straight both from front to back and from side to side.

"Guidon" or Lead File Rider

One rider needs to be the person to "dress on." If you watch an old John Wayne cavalry movie, like *She Wore a Yellow Ribbon*, you will see someone called a "guidon" who carries the unit flag at the far right of the group (fig. 7.10). This position is also known as the "lead file rider" because the whole unit takes direction, both side to side and front to back, from this person. In parades, just as in cavalry, the horse at the far right in the front row is naturally the guidon or lead file rider. She should concentrate on keeping the horses in the middle of your group's formation in the center of the street.

The "leader" of your group—see p. 106— should be the lead file rider whenever possible. If your group's leader is to ride in front of the rest of the riders, the riders behind him still need someone to dress on, in which case another individual should be chosen to fill the position.

Front-to-Back Dress

As mentioned, the dress starts with the lead file rider in the front right position. Each row "dresses" front to back on the person in front of them, keeping spacing between to 2 and 4 feet.

Side-to-Side Dress

"Dress right dress," is what they say in the mili-

7.10 In this photo from President Woodrow Wilson's review of the cavalry in maneuvers in 1913, you can see the "guidons" carrying the flags in the far right position of their units (right side of the photo).

tary. That means that each row dresses to the far right person to maintain side-to-side dress. This varies according to different needs. For crowd control, we police officers ride "boot to boot," as we are trying to create a "solid wall" to move a crowd. In a parade, however, you can "open" the line up. Just remember that the larger the gap between you, the harder it is to maintain consistent spacing. Keep it at no more than 2 feet, side to side (figs. 7.11 A–C). There are specific rules for this in cavalry manuals, but believe me, when the spacing is even, it will look good. Remember, your group dresses front to back, as well (see p. 114), so it is important that the front row riders space themselves apart correctly.

7.11 A–C Here you see a well-dressed column of four two-year-old police horses in training (A & B). The riders are dressed "boot to boot"—note there is little to no space between them. Remember, you dress from front to back, and from side to side, as demonstrated in the neat columns of two (C).

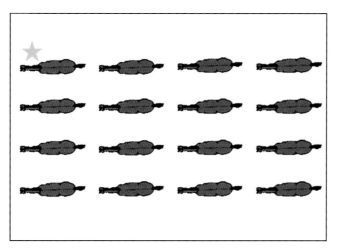

7.12   A column of four. The star denotes the "guidon" or lead file rider (see p. 114).

Parade Formation

In general, the easiest formation for riders to maintain is a straight line across. Riding in fours is easier than riding with larger numbers, like six or eight (fig. 7.12). If you have an odd number, maintain as much consistency as you can. Essentially, you want your pattern to look symmetrical to parade spectators. (I discuss the concept of formation at some length in the next chapter, p. 121.)

The Wedge

Typically, the wedge is a tactical formation for crowd control. It is not easy to maintain, so only use it in a parade if you have practiced. Start in a straight line across. You need at least six riders abreast to look good. The two riders in the center ride out, and then the next two align their horse's head with the center riders' boots. Then, the next two riders align the same way with each horse's head again at the leg of the rider just in front and to the right or left (fig. 7.14). And so on, depending on the number of horses in your

FLAG PROTOCOL

Dressing on the front right rider is important for flag protocol. When a rider carries the American flag, there should be "guards" flanking him on each side. Consequently, you need a minimum of three riders. When your group is carrying more than one flag, the hierarchy goes from right to left: American, state, county, and unit. When you are riding in fours (see fig. 7.12), the two front-and-center riders should carry flags—the Stars and Stripes on the right and a state flag on the left—with the two outside riders as the guards. When a group is presenting all four, there needs to be six riders abreast in order to include the two guards.

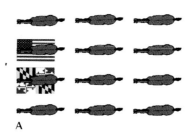

A

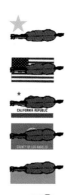

B

7.13 A & B   The proper way to carry two and four flags in a parade—shown in a column of four (A) and a column of six (B).

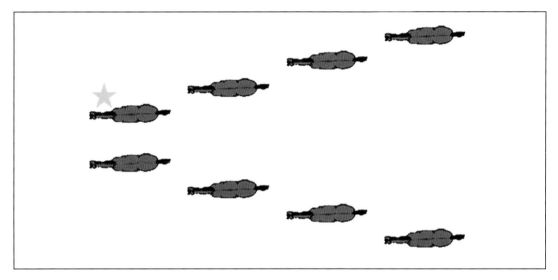

7.14 The wedge formation. The star denotes the "guidon" or lead file rider (see p. 114).

group. When you have an odd number of riders, the lone rider should take the place of the pair in front. (See more about the wedge formation in the next chapter, p. 121.)

Turn, Turn, Turn

Dressing on the front rider is easy when walking straight down the road, but what happens when the parade takes a turn? Turns of three or more horses are referred to as "wheels" or turns, and all wheel or turn commands typically mean 90 degrees. A turn of wheel "about," however, is 180 degrees. Think "U-turn," here (figs. 7.15 A–D). Technically, a wheel is a tighter maneuver; the pivot horse in a wheel actually does a turn on the forehand. The outside rider has the most distance to travel. The inside pivot horse risks turning so quickly that the outside rider cannot keep up. This means that the two riders need to make eye contact with one another. The riders in between can look to the

pivot, but they must be conscious of the outside horse's pace in order to keep the dress.

Most spectators won't know the difference between a wheel and a turn, and most parades are in a straight line, so don't worry about the terminology. Just dress right, keep your line straight, and watch your spacing.

Finishing Touches

Knowing some drill team or musical ride patterns can add professionalism and style to a mounted group in a parade. When the parade pauses, or when you find yourself in front of a reviewing stand, your group can perform one of these patterns to entertain and impress spectators—not to mention keep your horses busy. I explored drill team work to some extent in my first book, and I go into even greater detail in the next chapter (see p. 121). Together with what you've learned in these last pages, you'll be on your way to becoming a parade pro.

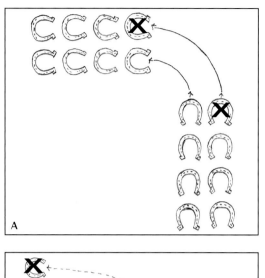

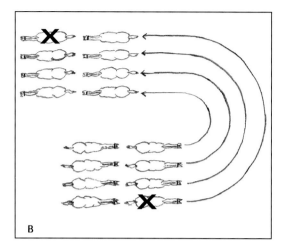

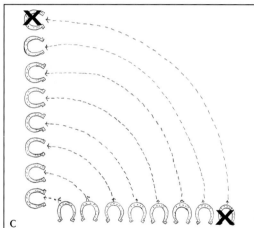

7.15 A–D To form a 90-degree turn (A) or U-turn (B), or the wheel when you have three or more in your line (C) the horses on the inside track move more slowly than those on the outside track. Remember to "dress right," meaning the horse on the outside (marked "X") sets the pace and the ones on the inside adjust accordingly. When your line is very long, as shown in C, the horse on the outside may be cantering while the inside horses are trotting or walking. Photo D demonstrates a group negotiating a mild turn in a local parade. The horses in the left column need to extend their pace slightly to maintain dress.

YOU'D HAVE TO HAVE SEEN IT TO BELIEVE IT: THE STORY OF MOUSE

Debbie Fuller was riding in one of our mounted police units in the Inaugural Parade in Washington, DC, on January 20, 2009, when her horse, Mouse, found himself in a quite a predicament. Mouse had decided to level a kick at a truck along the parade route. Well, the truck had a winch and a push bar on its grille, and much to his surprise and discomfort, Mouse got his foot stuck in the grille.

I was working security on the west side of the National Mall when a call came out for assistance. We were initially under the impression the horse had a broken leg, and Sergeant Chairs from Metro DC Mounted rushed to the scene. As it turned out, the vet was already there. He tranquilized Mouse so that the police could extract the horse's foot from the truck grille.

Amazingly, Mouse was fine except for a few scrapes, but he was in no shape to participate in the remainder of the parade.

7.15   Debbie Fuller and Mouse.

Sergeant Chairs escorted the famous Days End Farm horse ambulance—with Mouse aboard— back to the Prince George's County Equestrian Center. This story goes to show that you never can tell what might happen during a parade!

8

Drill Team Work and Musical Rides

Introduction

A *drill team* is a mounted group—known as a "unit"—riding in patterns to showcase aptitude and creativity. Just like synchronized skating or swimming, performing on horseback in varying configurations requires not only expertise but also clever choreography and the ability to work seamlessly with other individuals. A *musical ride* is a drill team presentation enhanced by the addition of a soundtrack. Of course, a well bombproofed horse focused on the job at hand is a huge advantage in either case.

Riding patterns also adds professionalism and style to any mounted group—in a parade, for example (see p. 103). When a parade pauses or your group finds itself in front of a reviewing stand, your team can entertain and impress spectators. You can also put on regular performances: state or county fairs, horse shows, and other gatherings are all opportunities for your drill team to gain some visibility and showcase its riding skills.

Studying the diagrams I provide throughout this chapter is crucial to your understanding. As you read about the various movements, look at the accompanying plan to see how each horse should travel.

Prerequisites

Rider Skills
Riders should be team players. That is, they should be able to follow orders. They must not be argumentative or have a need to debate decisions. They need to be able to concentrate, pay attention to their own position and others'

too, and recover from a mistake quickly without panicking.

Horse Skills

Reliability is the most important quality in a drill team mount. A nice-looking horse that moves well but gets nervous easily is less desirable then a horse that is dull but steady. Horses that kick and bite won't do, either. (You will find that strategic placement of horses within the unit can help decrease any occasional infighting.)

Bombproofing Skills

The horses in the unit should already be bombproofed to the extent that you feel comfortable taking them to a new location with unknown distractions. They should accept loud noise (which, in many cases, is music coming out of speakers or an announcer on the PA system) because, at times, you may have to ride very close to the source. Horses should accept visual stimuli from either side without shying. And, at any public performance, you may encounter kids with balloons, flapping tents and banners, and people moving and darting around, perhaps sometimes wielding umbrellas. The lead horses for each squad, in particular, must be able to move forward confidently, no matter what they see ahead.

Arena Size

Consider a standard dressage arena—20 by 40 meters in diameter—as the minimum size for an eight-horse ride. This translates into approximately 22 by 44 yards, or 66 by 132 feet. Obviously, a group with fewer horses can manage with less space, and larger groups need more. The Royal Canadian Mounted Police, who are famous for their group riding performances, use a 220- by 120-foot arena for 36 horses.

More importantly, your practice area should be a similar size to that in which you will per-

form. See p. 129 for instructions on how to set up a portable arena so your performance space is always the same size as your arena at home.

Drill Team Basics

There are a few terms that are necessary to know when putting together a drill team:

- ➤ *Unit:* All the members in your ride.
- ➤ *Squad:* One-half the members in your ride, divided by columns of twos and assigned numbers (see below). A team of eight riders would be broken into two squads of four: Squad One and Squad Two.
- ➤ *Squad Leaders:* Squad One's leader is Rider 1; Squad Two's leader is Rider 2.
- ➤ *Lead File Rider*: This is always Rider 1. She sets the pace and leads the entire unit (see also p. 114).

Numbering Riders in Columns of One or Two

In a single file line—called a Column of One—the number order is self-explanatory. The lead file rider is Rider 1, and you go on from there.

Riding in Columns of Two is a good starting formation for most movements. When breaking a unit into Columns of Two, you form two squads, one of even-numbered riders, and one of odd. For example, in a team of eight riders standing side by side in a straight line, the four riders on the right side (as you are sitting on the horse) are numbered Riders 1, 3, 5, and 7, and make up Squad One. Those on the left are Riders 2, 4, 6 and 8, and constitute Squad Two. The front right horse and rider is always Rider 1—the lead file rider.

The lead file rider leads Squad One as well as the entire unit, setting the pace and calling all commands. The only exception is when the squads are separated in a pattern, in which case Squad Two is led by Rider 2. (It is best to have your unit's riders memorize the ride so they can perform the movements without on-the-spot guidance.)

Maintain rider numerical order for all movements. When moving as squads, Squad One always goes first.

Spacing

Spacing between riders varies depending on the pattern. When riding in a single file column, you ride fairly close to one another—maybe half-a-horse's distance from tail to nose. When riding abreast (side by side) it is best to tighten up and ride "boot to boot," as we say. Each rider should make a habit of looking at her teammates and making small adjustments as needed to maintain spacing.

Use the standard rules of arena riding when riding in opposing directions: pass one another left shoulder to left shoulder. In addition, many movements require riders to ride *between* one another. (For examples, see Squad Crisscross, p. 125, and Thread the Needle, p. 126.) When this happens, you need to create enough space for horses to pass by, either beside you or in front of you. The importance is not so much the distance itself but rather that everybody in the unit leaves the same amount so the movement looks uniform. No one is going to take a measuring tape to check you, but the overall impression should be one of consistency.

When riding circles as a squad—or as unit—spread out evenly around the circle. When there are four riders, divide the circle into quarters. When there are eight, then eighths.

Gaits

In drill team, it is proper to sit the trot for most movements. Some are best performed at a walk—for example, when approaching head on in order to line up to make the Star (p. 124) or when entering the Pinwheel (p. 124). You may also do some cantering, such as in the Unit Circle (p. 124) or during the Thread the Needle (p. 126).

The Movements

The patterns I describe below build upon the formation work I discussed briefly in chapter 7 (see p. 116) and at more length in *Bombproof Your Horse*. They by no means constitute a comprehensive list of movements for drill teams but are simply meant to act as a starting point for you and your riding friends to design your own presentation.

With some patterns, I suggest a way to enter them; others are presented as stand-alone. When planning your program, you need to imagine how your unit will get into and out of each movement. There are endless different approaches and combinations.

The Unit Circle

The name says it all: The unit rides in a circle. If riding in a Column of One (see p. 122), it can be performed easily in numerical order or, Squad Two can follow Squad One (figs. 8.1 A & B). The only difference is the order of riders. This is a good movement to use for a moment of canter.

The Pinwheel

The Pinwheel requires Squads One and Two ride at the walk into the movement from opposite directions. When the lead riders from each squad are directly across from one another, the unit "rotates"—the spiral nature suggests a spinning pinwheel (figs. 8.2 A & B). Riders 1 and 2 must spin their horses very close together, without moving much forward, while the riders on the outside—Riders 4 and 8—must extend their stride or quicken their pace to cover more

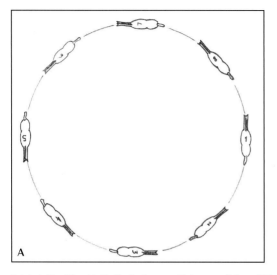 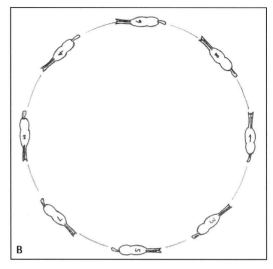

8.1 A & B The Unit Circle from a Column of One (A), and from Columns of Two with Squad Two following Squad One (B).

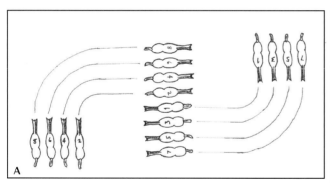 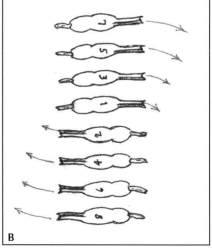

8.2 A & B Squads One and Two walking into the Pinwheel maneuver (A) and beginning to rotate as a unit (B).

ground. You can "spin" like this as many times as you'd like.

The Star

This movement has the two squads enter it at the walk from opposite sides of the arena until they meet, head to head, in the middle. All riders perform a turn on the forehand (see p. 53)—some to the right and some to the left—in order to spread out evenly and then do a "modified" side-pass (see p. 58) around the center of the "star" to make it "vibrate" (figs. 8.3 A & B). I say "modified" because you are moving around a circle, rather than along a straight horizontal line.

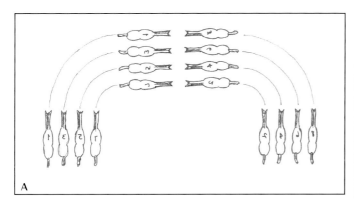
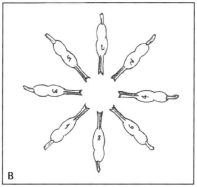

8.3 A & B   In the Star, the two squads walk toward each other from opposite ends of the arena until they meet head to head in the middle (A). Riders then use a turn on the forehand in one direction or the other to spread themselves out evenly and all perform a "modified" side-pass around the middle of the "star" at the same time (B).

The Star can be performed in two ways:

1   All riders make a "modified" side-pass in the same direction.
2   All side-pass in the same direction; halt; then return to their starting position by side-passing the opposite way.

In addition, there are two ways to exit the Star:

1   Return to the head-to-head starting position by reversing the entire procedure.
2   Rein-back all together, halt and turn on the forehand in the same direction so that you are in a circle, head to tail.

Squad Crisscross

When on opposite sides of the arena, both squads turn simultaneously from the track toward the middle, going from single file to abreast (called "flanking"), and ride toward, and then *between* each other (fig. 8.4). In order for the movement to be of visual interest to spectators, you need to pay special attention to keeping the spacing *even* as the squads pass

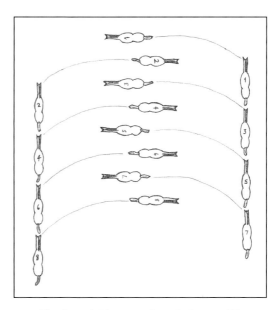

8.4   The Squad Crisscross: Squads One and Two turn toward each other from opposite sides of the arena and ride *between* each other.

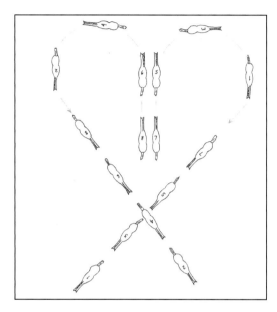

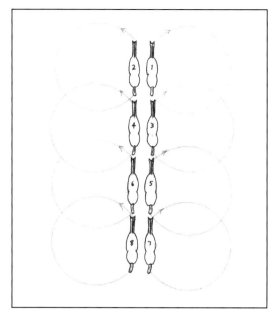

8.5   In Thread the Needle, Squads One and Two break from riding in Columns of Two down the centerline, turning away from each other and then riding diagonally across the arena to the other side. The squads intersect on the diagonal. The end pattern resembles the shape of a heart.

8.6   The entire unit performs Individual Circles from Columns of Two. Each rider performs her own circle, at the same time and the same size as the others.

by one another. If done properly, numbering becomes sequential during the moment the squads pass: Rider 2 rides between Riders 1 and 3, and so on.

Thread the Needle

In this movement, Squads One and Two ride a heart-shaped pattern. Starting from Columns of Two down the centerline, the squads split right and left to form the top of the heart, then ride diagonally toward the opposite side of the arena, intersecting at the bottom of the heart (fig. 8.5). Riders from each squad should alternate passing through the small spaces allowed by the columns.

Individual Circles from Columns of Two

The entire unit performs this simultaneously. Riding in Columns of Two, each rider makes her own individual circle: Riders in Squad One circle to the right, and those in Squad Two circle to the left (fig. 8.6). All riders should begin their circle at the same time and make it the same size as the others.

This is an easy movement to do while maintaining forward progress, which makes it a good fit for a short demonstration of a group's skill when riding in a parade (see chapter 7, p. 105).

Circles by Squad

In this movement, Squad One and Two ride in Columns of Two then split so each squad

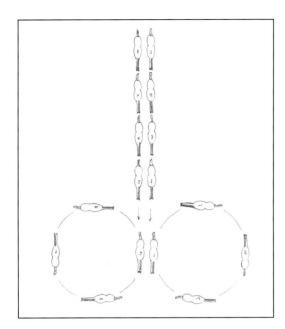

8.7   Circles by Squad is performed by beginning in Columns of Two, then splitting and each squad performing its own circle. The two circles should be adjacent and the same size—mirror images of each other.

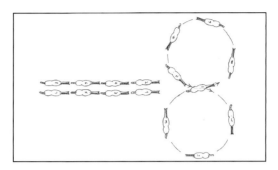

8.8   Squads One and Two can ride a Figure Eight by adjoining their adjacent Circles by Squad. Each rider, beginning with Rider 1, exits her squad's circle and enters the other squad's circle, riding between the other riders.

performs a circle (fig. 8.7). The horses should be spread evenly around the adjacent circles, with riders aligning with their column partners (Riders 1 and 2, 3 and 4, 5 and 6, 7 and 8, and so on). The circles should appear to be mirror images.

The Figure Eight

This classic movement is best performed after Circles by Squad (see above). Once each squad has established its circle, you merely change the timing slightly so that the adjacent circles intersect, and the entire unit rides a figure eight. This means that, beginning with Rider 1, the riders pass between each other and cross over from their circle to the other squad's circle (fig. 8.8).

The easiest way to exit the Figure Eight is to simply partner-up at the point where the two circles meet and ride ahead in Columns of Two.

Or, the lead rider can break the pattern and the unit can ride out in a Column of One (in numerical order, of course).

Individual Circles to the Centerline

Starting from both long sides, Squads One and Two simultaneously perform individual circles, momentarily meeting and riding next to their partner (Riders 1 and 2, 3 and 4, etc) close to the centerline before returning to the long side (fig. 8.9).

On Line

"On Line" is simply the term for lining up the entire unit abreast. The lead file rider makes the call and takes her position on the far right, and all other riders in the unit fall in line to her left (fig. 8.10).

The Wedge

The Wedge may be performed from the On Line formation (see above) or Columns of Two. The numbering of the riders differs depending on which of the two options you choose. Note: In either scenario your horse's head should be positioned just behind the leg of the rider in front of you.

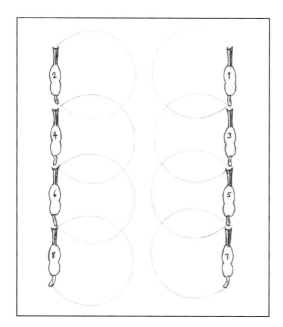

8.9   Individual Circles to the Centerline: Squads One and Two simultaneously perform individual circles on opposing long sides.

In addition, there are two ways to ride the Wedge once you begin:

1   Each person simply rides straight ahead or at an angle (figs. 8.11 A & B).
2   Riders on the right perform a left shoulder-in, and those on the left perform a right shoulder-in, giving the formation a more angled appearance (fig. 8.11 C).

Planning a Musical Ride

Now that you have mastered some drill team patterns, string them together into a complete performance. And why not add some music in the background? Audiences thrill at the sight of cadenced horses "dancing" to their own soundtrack.

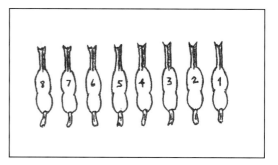

8.10   When a unit goes On Line, they line up side by side, beginning with Rider 1 on the far right.

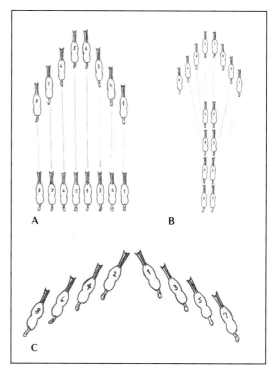

8.11 A–C   You can enter the Wedge from the On Line formation (A) or from Columns of Two (B). Once in position, you can either ride straight ahead or in a shoulder-in, to give the maneuver a more angled appearance (C).

As I mentioned earlier in the chapter, you must consider the space you will be performing in and use the same size area for practice (see p. 123 and sidebar). This is especially important with musical rides. If the performance area is smaller than your practice arena, your ride will likely be done before the music is over, and if larger, you'll still be riding after the music has finished. (Note: In a pinch, an easy way to make a program shorter or longer is by subtracting or adding circles.)

As with drill team work, the majority of the ride should be done at the sitting trot, but some movements are best performed at the walk. Reserve canter work for the larger patterns and for appropriate changes in the music (see more about gaits, timing, and music below). Once you have choreographed your ride, go through all the movements at the walk to help memorize the order, and when the group is sure of itself, instate the designated pace.

Music Selection

I suggest you use instrumental music only, and steer clear of vocals, which tend to distract an audience. You will probably need to choose several different pieces of music for your performance soundtrack; make sure they complement one another. For example, a classical selection followed by modern jazz could present too stark a contrast and again, just distract from rather than complement the performance.

The musical accompaniment should relate to how many steps per minute the unit's horses take at each gait. This translates to beats per minute, or BPM. According to the classic book on dressage to music *Dancing with Your Horse* (Half Halt Press, 2003), the average range of beats per minute for each gait are as follows:

- ➤ Walk: 50 to 66 BPM
- ➤ Trot: 76 to 88 BPM
- ➤ Canter: 96 to 108 BPM

MAKING A "PORTABLE ARENA"

You can use a variety of items to fashion a "portable arena" to ride in when you are performing away from home. This is a great way to be sure you use an area the same size as the one you practice in. Here's the quickest, easiest route to a proper arena wherever you may be:

1   Bring 14 ground poles—eight for the corners, and two each to place near the dressage letters C, B, and E. Your unit will enter at A, so no need for poles there.
2   You'll need traffic cones or potted plants (a more attractive option) to mark the letters and corners.
3   Use a measuring tape of adequate length and a can of spray paint (use just a "dot" of paint) as a guide to setting poles and markers. The standard dressage arena is 20 by 40 meters (about 66 by 132 feet). Make sure you leave a "buffer zone" of at least 10 feet between your arena edge and spectators.

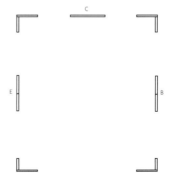

8.12   A visual guide to building your own "portable arena."

You can measure your horse's BPM with a stopwatch and by counting every time the inside front front foot strikes the ground for one minute. Similarly, you can figure out the BPM in a piece of music by tapping your foot to the downbeat while keeping an eye on your stopwatch.

In addition, you might find the following guide to time and distance offered by Werner Storl in his book *Riding to Music* (Breakthrough Publications, 1987) useful in planning your ride. This way, you can tell approximately how long you need a certain kind of music to last. Storl's estimates apply to a 20- by 40-meter arena.

	Walk	Trot	Canter
Whole Arena	60 seconds	35 seconds	25 seconds
20-Meter Circle	30 seconds	20 seconds	15 seconds
10-Meter Circle	15 seconds	10 seconds	5 seconds

Music Production and Sound System

You need a reliable sound system for practice, loud enough for all riders to hear, and you must be able to start and stop it as necessary from horseback. This means you either need a remote control or you need to position the equipment high enough and near enough to the arena that you can reach the dials. (Note: The speakers should be placed at least 10 feet away from your performance area so they don't scare the horses.) Alternatively, an assistant on the ground can help.

Consider the sound system when you are performing in front of an audience, as well. When the management of an event provides the equipment, check to make sure it is adequate for your purposes and that the person in charge of your music knows how to operate it in advance.

Your music needs to be burned to one compact disc (or "mixed" into one computer file) so it plays as a seamless piece. There isn't time to

PERFORMANCE TIPS

- Each rider in the unit should study a copy of the planned ride (see Sample Musical Ride, p. 131) before practicing on horseback.

- Once your riders have learned the ride and as the day of the performance approaches, practice *as if* you were performing—that is, when a rider makes a mistake, keep going. You will not get a "do-over" on the big day so learning how to recover on the fly is important.

- Warm up your horses for at least 10 minutes in the arena at some point prior to your ride. This acclimates them to the new setting and helps the riders in your unit get oriented.

- Remember to watch your own spacing and the other riders in the unit during the performance. *Even* spacing between riders is the sign of a professional performance.

- The lead file rider needs to maintain the correct pace during the performance. Riders tend to rush on performance day so she must keep timing *even*

change a disc in the middle of the ride. I advise producing your music with about two seconds of silence separating each new selection. Make at least two copies of your final music in case one is lost or damaged.

Sample Musical Ride

This program is an example of one way to organize the drill team movements I described earlier in this chapter. I've used a simple handwritten notation system to indicate which maneuvers to use at specific times. Each numbered arrow represents one rider's number. I've also use basic dressage arena letters for orientation. They have nothing to do with making a regulation-size dressage arena, but are simply there as reference points. When you "sketch out" your ride like this, don't worry about your notes being precisely to scale. Use them simply to organize your ideas.

1 Both squads enter in Columns of Two at the trot and split right and left at C. Continue down the long sides of the arena.

2 While on the long sides of the arena, members of both squads simultaneously circle inward. Lead file Rider 1 can signal that the turn is coming with a verbal command or by doing a slight shoulder-in. Each rider must make a circle. Squads pass each other in single file at A.

3 Riding down the long sides, each squad flanks (turns as a unit) toward the centerline. As the riders cross by each other, squads alternate by numerical order.

4 At B and E, the squads turn into single file and ride toward C.

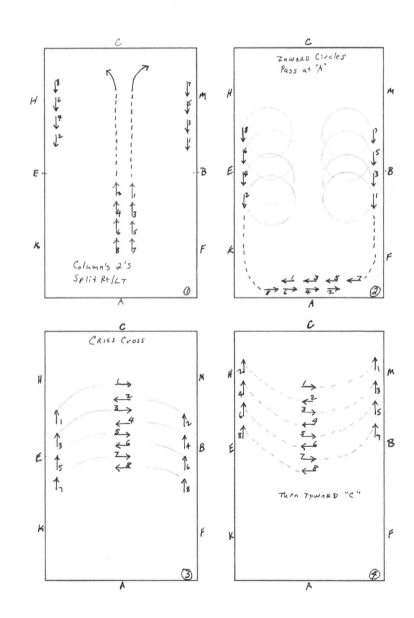

5   Riders meet down the centerline between H and M and move into a Column of One. Riders must give themselves room to blend into the line smoothly while creating space for the horse moving in the line in front of them. Meet at C between H and M. Resist the urge to meet abruptly at C.

6   Ride single file down centerline. Split left and right into squads at A. Squad One goes left and Squad Two goes right. Squads circle back to the centerline and meet in Columns of Two.

7   Columns of Twos ride down the centerline, and split right and left at C. Prepare for the next movement: Thread the Needle (see p. 126).

8   Perform a Thread the Needle across the diagonal to K and F. Squads pass single file at A.

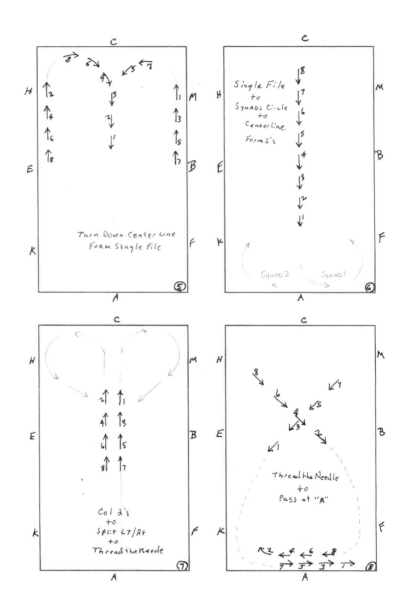

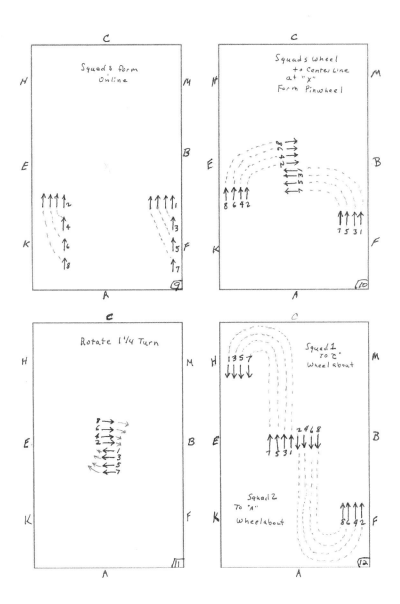

9   Squads proceed down long sides at first, then form On Line (see p. 127). Notice that Squad Two must cut the turn slightly to the inside to allow the rest of sSquad Two enough room to line up on the left of Rider 2. Rider 2 must stay off the rail to allow space. Go to a walk while going to On Line. Continue at a walk into the Pinwheel (see p. 124).

10   Squads wheel toward the center leaving "X" (the center letter) in between them. Notice that Squad Two needs to be slightly ahead of Squad One to coordinate a nice, crisp, simultaneous turn. Staying at the walk, form the Pinwheel.

11   While in the Pinwheel make a turn. Squad One will then be facing C, and Squad Two will be facing A. Continue to walk.

12   Squad One rides toward the C side and Squad Two rides toward the A side. Each squad will do a U-turn while still walking.

13   Squads wheel toward the center-line at B and E, and meet at X head to head. Remain at the walk.

14   Spread out to begin the Star (see p. 124). Rotate by passing in either direction or both. Rein-back.

15   Halt and turn on the forehand to the right forming a circle. The circle should be large enough to start out at the trot: on a signal from Rider 1, all riders trot from the halt—at the same time. Do not wait for the person in front of you to go. Make at least one trot circle, then go into can-ter. (Note: This is a good movement to add time when you need it—just make additional circles.) Follow Rider 1 out of circle at B.

16   While riding the turn between M and C, Squad Two must cut to the inside so the squads can form Columns of Two. The inside track that Squad Two is following is shorter than Squad One's, so they should be caught up by H. Continue Columns of Two down the long side.

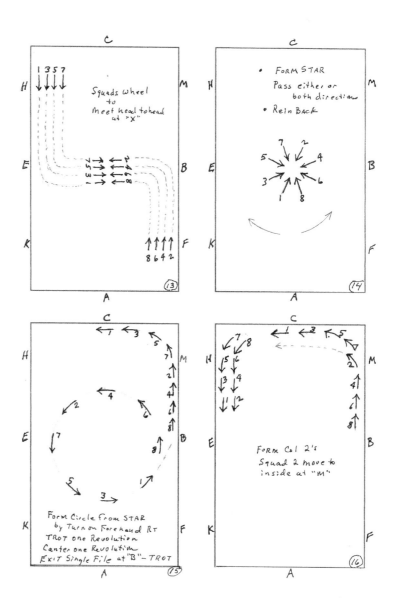

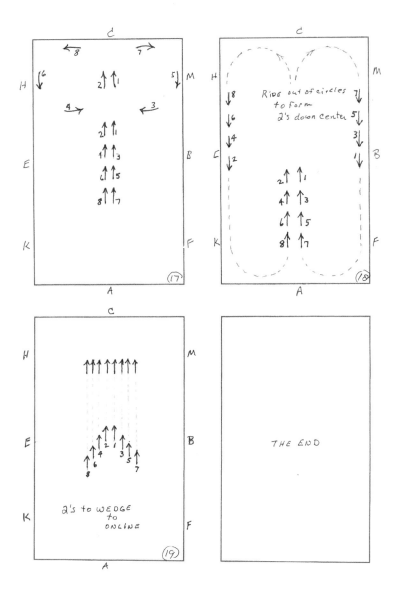

17   Columns of Two ride down the centerline at A. Squads circle between M and H. Again, make as many circles as necessary for the time allowed.

18   Each squad will exit the circles in single file with Squad One between M and B, and Squad Two between H and E. Meet at A between K and F, proceed down the centerline in Columns of Two.

19   From Columns of Two, transition to walk and form the Wedge (see p. 127). From the Wedge form On Line from the rear: Riders 7 and 8 catch up with Riders 5 and 6, then these four catch up with Riders 3 and 4. Finally, they join Riders 1 and 2.

20   Halt, salute.

9

Defensive Tactics for Trail Riders

Introduction

You are probably very accustomed to minimizing your risks when you are riding. You wear a helmet, you don't jump higher jumps than you should, and you keep away from horses with red ribbons in their tail. But, sometimes riders do let their guard down in regard to their personal safety. One place this commonly occurs is on the trail.

Trail riders should do their best to never ride alone. Take a friend with you when you can, or at the very least, let someone know where you are going and when you expect to return. When you do ride alone, don't go on a new or green horse—that "getting- to-know-you" trail ride should be taken in company. Make sure your mobile phone is charged, which you should

always bring, although many of the best trails are well out of range of wireless service. Keep your tack and your horse's shoes in good shape. Don't challenge yourself too much, either when exploring a new path or riding (i.e., don't be tempted to ride fast or jump).

Even when you take all these precautions, riding out can be dangerous: What we generally think of as urban crime—muggings, assaults, and thefts—all occur in remote areas, too. Criminals can lurk on country roads and a park's bridle paths, and prey on riders far from help. On the police force, we teach officers defensive tactics to effect arrests and to protect themselves. In the pages that follow, I've provided a version of our training. First I outline how it works on the force, and then I modify it for civilian riders.

The Use of Force Continuum

Police Rules

First, let's talk about the use of "force continuum," a standard that provides law-enforcement officers (and civilians) with guidelines as to how much force may be used in any given situation. As a police officer, I am obviously concerned that a desperate individual may hurt me during an altercation, but I must also be aware that the attacker may sue me later if he should be injured while I'm defending myself.

The force continuum model for the progressive use of force by the police goes like this:

- ➤ *Physical Presence*   Let's say a uniformed officer stops a person for a violation like jaywalking or entering a forbidden area. Often the officer's very presence is enough to encourage compliance with the law.
- ➤ *Verbal Commands*   These are orders such as, "Stop where you are," or "Put your hands up."
- ➤ *Empty Hand Techniques*   These include punches, kicks, holds, or arm locks.
- ➤ *Intermediate Weapons*   Pepper spray or mace, for example.
- ➤ *Deadly Force*   This includes use of a firearm, but also improper use of a night stick, such as a head strike. Deadly force is not condoned unless an officer is defending himself against an assailant who is himself armed with a deadly weapon. Before using any type of force, several things including the suspect's physical charateristics must be considered by the police. How big is he compared to the officer? What is the age difference? Physical disparities? Is he armed? The law takes all these into account after the fact if a complaint is filed.

Civilian Rules

Even though civilians are not strictly subject to force continuum rules, they need to make these same assessments before they take action against someone they perceive as threatening. For example, if a small woman is attacked by a large man, it is reasonable that she fear for her life, thus justifying deadly force. On the other hand, when a man defends himself (or counterattacks) and hurts a physically comparable assailant, he may have a harder time making his case. No matter how dire the situation seems "in the moment," you are responsible for the decision you make, and you may have to justify it in court.

However, you must not let this idea of responsibility stop you from defending yourself when necessary. The "use of force continuum" does not require you to always go through each step of the process—a life-threatening encounter can demand the immediate use of deadly force. An officer may not have the chance to find out if an assailant will respond to a verbal command. The point of understanding the continuum is to meet resistance with the force necessary to gain compliance when you're a police officer, and to make your safe escape when you are a civilian.

After the event, the process differs significantly for officer and civilian. Law enforcement officers never retreat from an attacker; in fact, they are obliged to stop the "bad guy" and make the arrest. Law enforcement officers only use force to stop an assault or make an arrest. Once the adverse action has ceased, so should the officer's use of force. This law applies to you, as well. If attacked, you should focus on halting or minimizing the attack in order to retreat from the attacker, not counterattack. (Note: If you are attacked in your home, the law recognizes that you have no obligation to retreat from the assailant, but can fight back with force.)

Defensive Riding

So how does all this understanding of the law of the use of force continuum keep you safer when riding trails? Know the regulations in your state and in any jurisdiction where you ride. If you use the horse you are riding to defend yourself against such an attack it may be viewed the same as if you had used an *intermediate weapon* such as pepper spray. Meanwhile, defending yourself from on top of your horse by using your feet or hands is considered equivalent to an *empty hand technique*—less "force" on the force continuum scale.

None of the defensive tactics I discuss in the pages that follow is 100-percent effective. Any attack can be countered—somebody can always find a way around any defense. The technique you should use depends upon where the assailant is, and how the situation unfolds.

The best line of defense, of course, is to avoid confrontation in the first place. As you ride, don't allow yourself to grow complacent. Don't develop "tunnel vision," even if you sense something is amiss and are bent on your escape strategy. You may focus on one person in front of you while others are hidden somewhere close by. Look behind you every once-in-a-while, as well, and don't ever wear headphones or chat on your cell phone. With music or a conversation added to the sound of your horse's hoof beats, you can be taken unaware very easily. Stay tuned in to your surroundings as you ride along.

If you see someone who seems suspicious or you get that "wary" feeling, obey your instincts. The easiest deterrent is to put distance between yourself and possible trouble. Move away quickly or maneuver so there is an obstacle between you—a tree, bush, rock, or creek will work fine. And remember: You're on horseback. If the person making you uncomfortable is on foot, you have the immediate advantage of being able to trot or canter away, and gain that safe distance far more quickly than you could if you were on foot.

The Horse as a Deterrent

When you are out alone and start to feel uncomfortable about a person approaching, do not—under any circumstance—allow him to pat your horse. When close enough to stroke your horse, he can easily pull the bridle off. Then, you really have a problem. We never allow a suspect to pat our horse, even during a standard traffic stop.

So let's imagine a scenario: An initially harmless looking jogger passes you, then turns and suddenly attacks. What should you do? You need to use your horse to "push" into the suspect, then get as far away as you can. Remember, every horse seems dauntingly powerful to a non-horseperson, and you have a number of options for self-defense with a well-bomb-proofed horse.

When thinking about how to use your horse as part of your self-defense strategy, visualize your vulnerable areas by imagining a heart-shaped barrier surrounding your horse's body (fig. 9.1). His head is at the top of the heart and his hind end at the bottom. The rider is most vulnerable if she allows a suspect into the heart area because both sides of the horse's head and neck are open to a grab for the bridle or reins. The heart-shaped barrier tapers at the rider's sides and the horse's hind end, indicating areas where the rider is again at advantage.

Moving the Hind End into the Attacker
It is always preferable to move the horse's hind end into the attacker; this reduces the chance of the suspect grabbing your reins or bridle and then controlling your horse (figs. 9.2 A & B). You can leg-yield (p. 44), side-pass (p.

9.1 Visualize a heart-shaped barrier surrounding your horse's body. The rider is most vulnerable when an attacker gets inside that barrier.

9.2 A & B Here we use a martial arts training shield to train Elliott to move his hind end into resistance.

58), perform a turn on the forehand (p. 53),or simply ride a small semi-circle in order to use the hindquarters as a deterrent. In the process, the suspect can be pushed away, stepped on, or struck by various parts of the horse, and then you are free to make your getaway as rapidly as you can.

Frontal Attack
When an attacker attempts to take control of your reins from the front, put your legs on your horse and drive him forward directly into the as-sailant (fig. 9.3). Then, using your aids, you can immediately follow up by:

- Leg-yielding the horse's hind end into the person.
- Neck-reining the horse's front end toward the person (fig. 9.4).
- Side-passing into the person.
- Neck-reining the horse into a turn on the forehand toward the person, so he is sud-denly faced with your horse's rear end and hind legs coming toward him in a threaten-ing manner.

9.3   Anne drives Elliott straight into the "assailant" who made an attempt to grab her reins from the front.

9.4   Using a martial arts training shield, we train Elliott to move his forehand into resistance.

Once your attacker is off balance—he will have moved to avoid being run over by your horse—you can get away. Remember, the movement(s) you use need not be "picture-perfect"; instead, they need to be far more dynamic and quicker than if you were taking an equitation test.

Side Attack

To reach you in the saddle, an attacker must gain control of your horse or simply pull you off, so he may try to pull down on your rein from the side. Should this occur, resist any temptation to snatch the rein back from him. His leveraged advantage from being on the ground will unseat you, *and* your arm will be available to him to use to pull you out of the saddle. Instead, release the rein completely and move your horse into him using a side-pass. (You see, all that schooling pays off, even in the most extreme situations.)

When an assailant attempts to pull you off by grabbing your arm, your lower leg on the side of the attack will probably move into the horse, prompting him to go sideways and result in you falling off. To counter, keep this foot in the stirrup and slightly away from the horse, which will force the assailant to pull against himself. Add pressure with your opposite leg to encourage the horse to move into the attacker (figs. 9.5 A–C).

Empty Hand Techniques

In the Saddle

I am only going to recommend one type of kick: the front kick. Do not attempt a side kick from horseback, since it will be weak at best; you don't have your usual balance when you are in a riding position. Also, a side kick gives the attacker an easy opportunity to grab your foot and push or pull you out of the saddle.

For you to use the front kick, the assailant needs to be close to your foot. Create a distrac-

9.5 A–C   In A, Jess is being pulled from the side. The assailant on the ground has the advantage. Notice Jess is "weighting" her stirrup by bringing her leg away from Ringo. This technique causes the assailant to pull Jess into the stirrup, rather than out of the saddle, which limits his advantage. In addition, Jess is side-passing Ringo into the attacker. In B, Anne demonstrates the same technique on Elliott, a taller horse. She takes her right leg away from the horse, "weighting" the stirrup, which changes the angle of the force. Her left leg pushes Elliott into the assailant. In C Anne brings her leg forward, directing it toward the suspect. To do this, she sits up straight and lets the attacker pull her while she pushes Elliott into him with the opposite leg.

tion by engaging him in conversation so he is looking up at you. Then deliver the kick with the tip of your boot right to the center of his upper body (fig. 9.6). If it is delivered correctly, making contact anywhere near his solar plexus—the network of nerves situated in the abdomen—this kick will knock the wind out of him. I've seen the technique work in police crowd-control situations, so I can attest to its effectiveness.

Before attempting the front kick, however, consider the following. How tall is your attacker in relation to the horse you are riding? Where is your foot in relation to him? If for any reason the suspect attempts to *push up* on your leg to unseat you, let your leg go limp. Abandon your natural instinct to grip. When he pushes on you, but finds there is nothing to push, you have neutralized the attack (figs. 9.7 A & B).

9.6   Jess is in position to deliver a front kick to her attacker.

142

9.7 A & B Jess lets her leg go limp so the assailant has nothing to push against while simultaneously swinging Ringo's hind end into the attacker.

Let's imagine you are in a situation in which you are able to deliver a blow with your hands. In this scenario, you need to aim for one of the clusters of nerves called "pressure points," which are all over the human body. You have most likely banged your elbow and felt that electrified sensation up and down the arm (your "funny bone"), or gotten a "Charley horse" from banging your thigh into something hard. These are examples of pressure points in action.

Here are a few methods that allow even a small person to deliver an effective blow by taking advantage of those pressure points (figs. 9.8 A & B). You can also use these techniques from the ground should the need arise. Note: When on a tall horse, it is less likely you will be in the right position to deliver these effectively.

➤ An open hand slap to the ears.
➤ A blow delivered to the side of the neck with either the forearm, closed fist, or side of the hand.

➤ A palm strike to the nose.
➤ Repeated strikes to the top of the suspect's forearm to cause his grip to loosen.
➤ Strikes to the back of the hand with just one or all your knuckles, or with the butt end of your crop (see below).
➤ Repeated blows to the front of the shoulder to temporarily weaken his arm.
➤ A pinch to the back of the triceps (muscle along the back of the arm).

Intermediate Weapons

Although, as I mentioned, the horse might actually be considered an intermediate weapon in some cases, I am not considering that to be the case here. Rather, we'll talk about the other most likely self-defense mechanisms an individual who rides on her own might employ.

Riding Crop or Whip

Unfortunately for riders who carry one, a crop is not a very effective weapon. As I said on

9.8 A & B Ringo is short enough to allow Jess to deliver empty hand strikes to an assailant. Here you see a closed-fist, hammer strike to the side of the neck (A). Notice she does not have to bend over to deliver it, which would put her off balance. In a situation like this, follow up by moving the horse into the assailant with one of the techniques discussed on p. 140. Jess delivers another fist strike to the top of the assailant's forearm (B). When used, this strike should be delivered in repeated blows to "fire up" the nerves in the arm and hand. This will weaken the attacker's grip.

p. 143, you can use the butt end of a crop to fire up a pressure point and enhance a hand strike, but more than likely, a riding crop will only irritate the attacker rather than deter him (figs. 9.9 A & B).

Pepper Spray

If you often ride alone or in new areas, you may want to invest in some pepper spray, which is a good intermediate weapon for riders since it's both compact and effective. Carry it on your belt in a holster—it will do you little good tucked away in a saddle bag—and you must practice so you know what to expect if you need to use it. Note: Check all local laws before purchasing or using pepper spray. Your area police officers will know which self-defense items you can carry legally.

As mentioned, pepper spray is very effective, as long as you know how to deploy it and are willing to endure the consequences—you will have at least "incidental contact" with the spray, which means that you will breathe some of it in yourself.

All law enforcement officers are intentionally exposed to pepper spray before they are issued any to use. This way, we aren't so surprised by its effects. I have also had incidental contact to pepper spray. I was once in a crowd-control situation when an officer sprayed it over my shoulder. It stung, and was mildly irritating, but I was not totally debilitated. Since then I have seen it used many times, and I've used it myself. In all my experience, I have never seen a horse adversely affected. Mostly they just give a snort or two to clear their nostrils. (By the way, horses are not affected at all by tear gas either.) Some people, too, are less bothered, and can still be combative, so don't expect pepper spray to be a magic bullet. Plan to use it only to buy you time to escape.

There are various types of pepper spray, which is actually made of *oleoresin capsicum*,

9.9 A & B   Anne demonstrates leveling a strike to the forearm of an assailant using the butt end of her whip.

or "really hot chili pepper." It can be purchased online or at hardware and sporting goods stores. In spray form, *oleoresin capsicum* is an inflammatory that causes difficulty breathing; coughing; and irritation of the eyes and nose, all of which can render someone unable to maintain an assault.

The four methods of using pepper spray are by stream, cone, fog, and foam. From horseback, stream is the best choice because it discharges easily, almost like water from a squirt gun, and it makes very little noise. The cone, which produces a cone-shaped discharge, is usually a little louder than the stream, and sometimes the noise and visual can affect the horse. Using this type requires some habituation.

In either case, choose a make of pepper spray that offers a can containing an inert option for training purposes. This means it is just propellant with water, and you can use this to safely and progressively train your horse to

accept it (figs. 9.10 A–C). It is also valuable for you, as you learn how much pressure you need to deploy the real spray. You can even substitute aerosol string—a.k.a. Silly String™ and available at party supply stores—for the inert spray (figs. 9.11 A & B). This makes for a fun way to desensitize your horse to the noise and sight of a substance in spray form, but without the cost of the inert canisters.

Most pepper sprays are discharged by depressing the activator with a thumb or index finger. You can keep one hand on the spray and the other on the reins, or you can hold the reins with both hands and discharge it with a finger. When an assailant enters the heart-shaped area I mentioned on p. 140, point the spray just below his face and then bring it up. Aiming at the face first often results in a discharge that's too high, in which case the spray wafts harmlessly away and accomplishes little other than enraging your attacker. It is better to aim low:

Even if you hit the assailant's chest, the spray will have some of the desired effect as it will rapidly spread up toward his eyes and nose.

Discharge the spray in one-to-two-second bursts until the dispenser is empty. Most canisters empty quickly after only a few bursts. Move away from the assailant as you discharge, and be sure not to ride into the cloud, or you will be exposed.

In summary, your best option for mounted self-defense is to *use your horse*. He offers both your most effective weapon and your best chance for escape. His ability to help you goes back to his bombproofing schooling, and his ability to move both forward and laterally at your command (see chapter 3, p. 37).

9.10 A–C   Here we are training Elliott and Ringo to the sound and visual effect of cone-type pepper spray, which makes a hissing sound and produces a wide stream (A). We start with the two horses equally distant and keep them walking because I like to keep their feet moving when first introducing spray. I have an inert can in each hand, and I discharge the spray behind my back to lessen the stimulus. Next, Anne and Jess spray me (the "assailant") from the saddle (B). Note Ringo's reaction, indicating he needs more training. Later, Anne deploys pepper spray from the saddle while Elliott holds his ground—a bombproof success (C).

9.11 A & B   I desensitize Guy to the sound and sight of a substance in spray form by discharging the aerosol string from the saddle (A). I aim it ahead at an angle, and toward the ground. Then Anne practices aiming and firing at an assailant—me (B)!

DECONTAMINATION

It is important to properly dispense of a pepper spray canister after use, even if you did not empty it. It will have pepper all over it, and can spread the stinging substance to your body and clothes.

The effects of pepper spray last for 30 to 45 minutes. When you've come into contact with it during an attack, open your eyes as soon as possible, and blink a lot. Try to keep your eyes open so they tear and flush themselves. Then, decontaminate with the following methods as soon as you return to the barn:

- Remove all sprayed clothing.
- Scrub your hands with soap at least three times before you touch anything else. Specialty washes are available for decontamination, but plain mild soap and shampoo are effective.
- Take out contact lenses if you wear them. Hard, clear lenses can be cleaned and used again. Soft "disposables" must be discarded.
- Use a stream of cool water from a spray bottle, garden hose, or kitchen faucet, or immerse your head in a bucket of water to flush your eyes.
- Wash any residue off your skin with water and soap. (You must rewash your hands often during this process to avoid recontamination.)
- Pat your skin with a wet paper towel, and then pat with dry paper towel. Repeat six to eight times to remove the resin.

10

Bombproofing for Kids

Introduction

It is often our hope that our kids' horses are *already* bombproof, but in reality, that is rarely the case. Fortunately, children and teenagers are completely capable of participating in this kind of training, and they are likely to have fun doing it.

This chapter will be most useful to instructors or parents, each of whom will have slightly different perspectives and expectations when a child or teenager has attained a high enough level of riding to begin bombproofing his or her horse or pony. I use all the same techniques with kids that I do with adults—I just communicate in a different manner (fig. 10.1).

Rules for Teaching Safe and Effective Riding

Instructors: Ride That Horse

The best advice that I can give an instructor is to *know* the horse your young student is riding. You must ride him yourself—unless of course, he is a pony and you are too heavy for him (fig. 10.2). I have had several students tell me they appreciate it that I ride their horse to gain some perspective on their experiences. Frankly, I'm surprised when I hear how many instructors out there never ride their students' horses. How do they know if the problem lies with the horse or the rider?

10.2   Whenever possible, I try to ride my students' horses so I can understand them and help my students ride them better. Here I am on Yogi, who belongs to my teenaged student, Alanna.

10.1   Younger riders, like my student Alanna, are capable of learning how to properly bombproof their horses. I use the same methods as I use with adults, including emphasis on basic schooling exercises (see chapter 3, p. 37). These are skills they will use for the rest of their riding life.

One of my teenagers was having a hard time getting anything out of her horse as we worked on leg-yielding. So I got on to see how responsive the horse was. Not very! I had to put my spurs on, and I got the best response when I was leg-yielding him on a tight circle. My student's previous instructor had never got on the horse, and she simply told my student the horse's unresponsiveness was due to the girl's leg not being strong enough. Sure, her leg wasn't as strong as mine, for example, but if I need spurs to get even a slight semblance of a response from a horse, then there was more to the equation than a lack of leg.

Because stories like this can often be the norm, when I first start working with young riders in basic dressage, I watch them ride at various gaits and movements to see what is going on. If a student is obviously following my instructions, but can't seem to get the horse to respond, I then get on the horse to see what is happening.

I teach cops how to ride; they do not respect an instructor who can't practice what he preaches. When a problem arises, put yourself in your student's saddle. Your student—and her horse—will appreciate your efforts.

In addition, remember that when teaching kids, in particular, demonstrating goes a long way. I have found you can discuss riding theory with adults and they will often be attentive, but kids will only listen for a short time. So show them instead! Keep the attention span issue in mind, and during a bombproofing lesson, keep things interesting and moving along.

PROOF

A mounted officer (and trainer) I knew casually called me one day and said he was in some kind of jam. He was being removed from his position and reassigned, and he wanted me to vouch for him—to write something up confirming his abilities. I had never actually seen him ride a horse, so I told him to come and do a riding evaluation on my own horse, and we would videotape it.

My horse at the time was a retired police horse named Scotty. He was a Thoroughbred-Quarter Horse cross and former eventer. The officers had nicknamed him "Rocket J. Squirrel" because of his quickness. He could be a bit challenging for a new rider, but I wasn't concerned. After all, this guy was a trainer, right?

Well, this fellow passed the mounting part of the review, and that was it. He wasn't able to trot any semblance of a circle, and Scotty was high and hollow and trying to run off almost immediately. I stopped things pretty quickly, and said I couldn't help him. His attorney called me about a week later, and I had to explain that his client was at best an advanced beginner—and that was generous. There was nothing else I could say.

The point of this story is that "show me" is one of the most important parts of good instruction. This officer was a good speaker, and he talked a good game, but it was all a sham. He could barely ride, never mind teach others. I suspect he had complaints from his fellow officers because of his inexperience. Last I heard, he had resigned from the force.

Different Learning Styles

When it comes to teaching riding, the question is whether the student can learn certain skills from the teacher's method of instruction. Students learn riding skills in different ways: through books, classroom instruction, demonstration, and actual riding. Any athletic skill must be demonstrated in order to be taught, but remember, with riding, to make things more complex, there are actually *two* students: the rider and the horse.

Foolhardiness vs. Fearlessness

Usually, kids are brave and ready to try anything without worrying about the consequences. So as instructors, we need sometimes to curb this natural enthusiasm and harness the energy so that training is productive for both horse and rider.

I have seen a few children lose confidence after a fall, or when switching to a more difficult horse. A more challenging horse is, of course, necessary to advance in riding skills, but if the horse is too difficult, the young rider may regress, or even give up riding altogether.

Proper Parental Support

Parents: Please remember you are there to help guide your children, not force them, into activities. When they express an interest in riding, be there to support them, and set them up for success. You can't ride the horse for them. You also can't nag them into giving a better performance. Too many parents live vicariously through their children, something we often see with team sports like football or baseball, and individual sports such as tennis. We've all heard stories of the over-invested parent fighting with the referee or coach. I see less of that sort of combativeness in the horse world, but it is there nonetheless.

Remember that the best horse for your child is the one she can handle (fig. 10.3). Don't get talked into buying a horse because he is

10.3   The best horse for your child is one she can handle. She should feel confident and capable, even when working over and through "scary" obstacles on a bombproofing course.

Keep It Fun

To build confidence and improve skills, try to make riding fun. Not all kids respond to competitive situations the same way. Don't get me wrong; I feel competition is a valuable aspect of teaching children, because if they aren't prepared to compete when they become adults, they will have a hard time in a professional situation. Most jobs have some element of performance expectation. When every kid "wins" a ribbon, regardless of how they performed, how does that serve to prepare them for real world challenges?

Watch for signs, however, of the stress of competition becoming too great. I had a friend whose daughter was a competitive swimmer for most of her childhood. She was excellent, but by the time she was offered a swimming scholarship at a university, she was burned out and declined it.

Some kids don't handle competition well at all, while others take it in stride for what it is. My daughter, for example, was on the swim team strictly for the social aspect. If she won something, great; if not, it wasn't a big deal. My son, on the other hand, didn't take losing very well. So I always left him the option of quitting swim team. But for him that was not an option. He stayed on the team even though he was aggravated much of the time. Then, there was the nightmare of baseball, where he was a backup pitcher. Talk about pressure. Couldn't he make things easy and just say, "I don't want to pitch anymore"? Nope.

Having had these trying experiences as a parent myself, I understand the fine line a parent has to walk. With riding, however, safety must come first. A child pushed to compete on horseback beyond her limits can get hurt. And, those told to compete when they'd rather be trail riding will eventually be turned off horses. Always, always, strive to keep riding safe and fun (figs. 10.4 A & B).

a good mover, or because he is cute. Instead, make sure your child is able to perform on that horse at the level she is currently riding. When your child can ride a basic walk, trot, canter, and jump a small fence, her horse should be able to do the same. If you have to re-school the horse so he goes safely for your child, you have wasted time, money, and energy.

If the child is having serious problems with a specific horse, you may need to move on to another one. Whatever you do, be very careful about "trading up" to a more difficult horse. Yes, your child will outgrow that little pony. But be sure she can handle the new prospect. It's natural for instructors to want their students to ride more difficult horses in order to advance and learn. However, the desire to progress does not mean that a horse should strike fear in the rider. *Riding* difficult horses and *buying* them are two entirely different scenarios. I've seen the frustration and aggravation kids go through when they own a "problem horse." Please don't get pushed into that situation.

10.4 A & B It should be a parent's number-one goal to keep riding safe and fun for his or her kids. A quiet, patient mount that your child is confident handling and that is a saint on the trails will go a long way in ensuring this goal is met.

The Pony Factor

When you're around kids who ride, you are bound to deal with the "pony factor" (fig. 10.5). Ponies are, by definition, equines that stand shorter than 14.2 hands. However, the term "polo pony" is used to describe a much taller horse that happens to play polo, and there are some examples of horse breeds—like Arabians or Morgans—that often don't quite make the 14.2-hand mark, but are nonetheless considered horses. The Icelandic Horse, which although short in stature, is not judged to be a pony by some, and of course the Miniature Horse, while easily smaller than most ponies, is again, not considered one of them.

10.5 When teaching kids to ride, you'll be teaching their ponies, too. Although cute, ponies often have a set of tricks up their sleeve; you need to be prepared to deal with potential "pony behavior."

Confusing, isn't it? Actually, the difference between ponies and horses is also in their build as well as their height. Ponies are often sturdier and stockier in proportion to their height than horses. They are also very strong. While a Shire, an enormous breed of horse, can pull his own weight, a little Shetland pony can pull *twice* his own weight.

Ponies look so cute that people often mistakenly believe they are easier to deal with than their larger equine counterparts. On the con-

trary, when a pony exhibits unruly behavior and it isn't dealt with effectively, the trouble snowballs. Ponies have a reputation for being very smart, mischievous, and devious. Sound training helps to prevent them from taking advantage of their riders.

Because of ponies' relative strength to their size, a trainer must take into consideration that

10.6   When working with a pony and his rider, treat groundwork the same as you would with a full-size horse. Handling the pony from the ground can actually be more challenging because of his strength and build.

groundwork may be actually harder with a pony than with, for example, a Thoroughbred (fig. 10.6). Don't be lulled into thinking, "It's just a pony." A pony's lower center of gravity means even an adult may have difficulty managing him, never mind a small child. In chapter 6 (p. 94), I discussed working with restraints over

the horse's nose to encourage forward movement and compliance. However, even with such tack, you may find yourself pulled around by a willful pony.

An older, experienced horse is often a better choice. Just be sure to size the horse to the rider so that the child can control her mount.

10.7   A great example of a rider successfully bombproofing her pony, and having fun while doing it!

Bombproofing Games

Introduction

Games are an excellent way for both child and grown riders to gain skills and increase their experience on horseback. Not only do you use the various schooling exercises I explained in chapter 3 (p. 37), but your horse also becomes accustomed to props (such as balls and flags), loud outbursts of cheering or clapping, and the pulsing adrenalin related to a group of horses running around an arena together. Games can also be a welcome break from the usual "work" associated with the riding ring.

In this chapter, I've outlined some of the best games I have collected and taught over the years. There are many variations of these games, and making up your own versions can be part of the fun—but to get you started I detail a simple way to play each one. Just be sure that all participants agree on the rules before you begin.

When planning a game, take into account the riding levels of your players. When beginners are involved, games should be played at the walk; however, a group of more advanced riders might enjoy a brisk canter during a bout of Capture the Flag in a wide-open field (see p. 158). Adjust the gaits used and intensity of the play accordingly.

Lead Line Relay Race

Two teams of riders begin from a start line at the *same* end of an arena. Across from the start line at the opposite end, two lead lines are draped over the top rail for easy access. The first rider from each team rides to the opposite end,

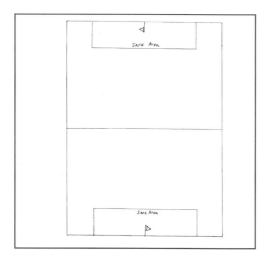

11.1 Capture the Flag

grabs a lead line, rides back to her team, and hands it off to the second rider. This rider then returns the line to the opposite fence. The relay is repeated until all the team's members have taken a turn riding and handing off a line. The team that finishes the process first wins.

Rules

You can use any number of riders on a team, but remember the location of the "finish line" will vary depending whether there are an odd or even number of riders. Sometimes the finish will be returning with the lead line in hand, while other times the game will end when the last rider replaces the lead rope on the fence. If the line falls to the ground at any point in transfer, the rider involved must dismount to replace it.

Space Required

You can have a relay race in almost any size area, as long as there is enough room to ride across and back. Even a round pen can offer enough room for a relay race with four or six beginner riders.

Improved Horse and Rider Skills

Relay races improve the horse's attentiveness, respect for rider control, and neck-reining ability.

Capture the Flag

Riders divide into two teams. The arena is split into two territories with a "home base," one for each team (fig. 11.1). In each territory, a "flag" or some other marker is posted in a way that is fairly easy to move—I use a lead rope, for example, draped over the fence at the end of each team's territory. The goal is for the riders on each team to attempt to "capture" the other team's flag from its base—while avoiding being tagged. If a rider brings the other team's flag back to her home base, her team wins.

Rules

If a rider is tagged as she attempts to obtain the opposing team's flag, she must remain in a "penalty box" in the opposing team's side of the arena for a predetermined time, such as 30 seconds or a minute. Here are some common variations of the penalty:

- Instead of sending the tagged player to a penalty box in the opposition's territory, send her back to her home side.

- You can free your teammates from the penalty box by tagging them. Let's say Team A has a captured member of Team B in their penalty box. If another Team B rider can reach the penalty box without being tagged, she can free her captured teammate.

- The tagged person has to dismount and return to her team's territory and then remount after a specified time limit.

A word of caution: Use a one-handed tag, and tag *riders only*. You don't want the game to evolve into an unsafe contest of smacking each other's horses. (To emphasize this point, you can make horse-slapping a penalty.)

Space Required

One of the advantages of Capture the Flag is that it can be played in any size area. In a small space, such as a riding arena, you would divide the arena in half for two territories, and designate two corners as "penalty boxes." More advanced riders can play in a wooded area, open fields, or in any other space that has safe footing and can be divided.

Improved Horse and Rider Skills

Capture the Flag demands maneuverability as you attempt to evade opposing team members, and the ability to change directions swiftly while being pursued. Also, the horse has to accept a rider carrying a "flag," whatever it may be.

Mounted Football

The goal of Mounted Football is to score points by advancing the ball into the opposing team's end zone (fig. 11.2). The ball can be advanced by carrying it or by throwing it to a teammate. Players score by carrying the ball over the opposing team's goal line, catching a pass thrown over that line, or tagging the other team's player when he has the ball. The winner is the team with the most points when the game is over.

Obviously, football has endless variations, but I will give you some basics based upon the version we play in the police department.

Rules

Use a foam football that will not hurt the horses or riders if they are hit with it. Decide which

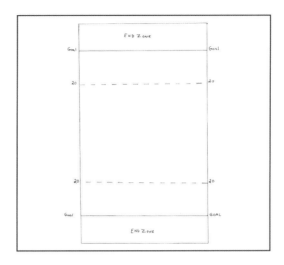

11.2   Mounted Football

team starts in the offensive position by flipping a coin. Each team lines up on opposing sides of the "scrimmage" line.

The quarterback begins the game holding the ball. Once she says, "Hike," the ball is in play. Most football games require a count of, say, "five Mississippi" before the defense can cross the line of scrimmage and go for the ball. Unlike in real football (where the quarterback can run), the quarterback in this game must pass the ball to a player on her team. Then, her teammates must try to pass the ball progressively down the field in order to score a touchdown. Members of the opposing team (the defense) try to prevent a score by tagging the player with the ball.

A game of mounted football begins with four "downs," or four chances to move the ball into the next zone (see p. 160). After four attempts, you must turn over the ball to the other team unless one of two things happens:

1   Your team completes three passes.
2   Someone on your team crosses into the next zone (see p. 160) holding the ball.

When either of these occurs, your team gets four more chances, also called "a first down." Some other general rules:

- A touchdown scores six points. (It is easiest to forget the "extra point" rule when playing football on horseback.)
- If the person with the ball drops it, the ball automatically goes to the other team.

Space Required

We play in an 80- by120-foot field, but you do not need the same space. There simply needs to be enough room to divide the arena to make a football field. You need to cordon the playing field into two or three zones. (I use dressage letters for this.)

Let's say you have an open area 150 feet long. Use 15 feet on each end for each team's end zone. This leaves you with a 120-foot playing field. Divide this into two 60-foot zones, or three 40-foot zones.

Improved Horse and Rider Skills

The main skill the riders need to play mounted football is the ability to ride with one hand, as you need the other hand for throwing, tagging, and catching. You will likely have to switch hands as well. If you catch with both hands, you need to act quickly to pick your reins up right away after you have caught the ball.

The horse must be conditioned to accept the ball being thrown to the rider or in his direction, as well as allowing the rider to throw the ball (this can involve a strange sensation of motion on his back). To work on this, desensitize your horse by starting on the ground beside him, petting him with the ball and throwing it up in the air and catching it. Next, mount up and have a person on the ground hand the ball to you, then hand it back to her. Ask your assistant to gradually

move farther away, until soon you are throwing the ball to and fro without upsetting your horse. Finally, get a buddy on horseback and, again, starting close, pass the ball back and forth until you can both toss and catch the ball from the saddle with your horses remaining calm (figs. 11.3 A–C).

Broom Polo

This is a lighthearted version of polo, best played on a calm day. Divide a group of riders into two teams. Each rider must be armed with a "mallet" (a broom). The object is to score goals by driving a beach ball over a line or through a goal on the opposing team's side of the arena or playing field.

Rules

This is a straightforward game with plenty of latitude. You can set the rules so that if the beach ball touches the opposite side of the arena or wall, it counts as a point, or you can make it harder by constructing an actual "goal" that players must hit the ball into.

Space Required

As long as both sides have the same amount of space, the needs for broom polo are widely variable.

Improved Horse and Rider Skills

Broom polo builds riding and bombproofing skills because the horse needs to grow accustomed to brooms—both his rider's and those of the other players—swinging about his body and his head. Also, the rider has to ride with one hand, improving both her and her horse's neck-reining ability.

11.3 A–C   For games like Mounted Football and Jousting (see p. 160), you should desensitize your horse to balls being thrown near him, and possibly hitting him. Begin on the ground by rubbing and tossing the ball against his body (A). Then mount up and ask an assistant to toss a ball back and forth with you, gradually increasing the distance (B). Graduate to throwing a ball back and forth with another rider (C).

Jousting with Foam Balls or Water Balloons

This game harkens back to medieval times and is based upon the martial arts skill of two mounted knights battling each other with lances in a competition setting. Instead, two modern-day riders trot or canter toward each other, "firing" foam balls or water balloons across a divider when within striking distance. The water balloons can be especially refreshing on hot summer afternoons.

The Rules

At a signal given by a non-mounted participant, two riders trot or canter toward one another, passing left shoulder to left shoulder on opposing sides of a "tilt," or barrier, as in the tradition for jousting. As they pass, they attempt to hit one another—not the horse—with either a foam ball or water balloon (figs. 11.4 A–C).

Space Required

You need a jousting lane long enough so the horses can get up some speed, but short enough so that the "knights" are not spending too much time riding toward each other, and the game maintains some sense of immediacy. A dressage or schooling arena works well. Fashion a "tilt" with some jump standards and rope, or use another rudimentary barrier such as a line of traffic cones—you just need to separate the two sides to lessen the chance of the horses running into one another.

Improved Horse and Rider Skills

To "joust," a horse needs to be conditioned to ride directly toward another with only a narrow barrier separating them. He also needs to get used to a ball or balloon being thrown at him—the horse doesn't know that it is being aimed at the rider. (See p. 160 for steps to condition

11.4 A–C To "joust," construct a "tilt" or barrier down the middle of your arena (A). Line up on the opposite end as your opponent, and trot or canter toward her (B). When you meet, shoulder to shoulder, "fire" your foam balls or water balloons at her (C).

a horse to ball sports.) Water balloons add an extra desensitizing challenge, since they pop and release water upon contact.

PHOTO AND ILLUSTRATION CREDITS

All photos by Eliza McGraw except: figs. 2.1, 2.7 A & B, 2.9, 2.11 A–F, 3.8, 3.12 A & B, 3.15 B–E, 3.17, 3.18 A & B, 3.20 A–F, 4.7 A–D, 5.3 A–N, 6.5, 6.6 A–C, 6.7 A–H, 6.9, 7.3, (Jenifer Boccia Werts); fig. 2.5 (Rick Pelicano); figs. 2.19 A–C, 3.5, 3.22 A–H, 3.24, 4.4 A, 4.8, 7.2, 7.6 B, 7.11 A–C (Asbury Police Mounts); figs. 2.20 A & B, 4.4 B, 4.5 A & B, 4.9 A–C (Wilma and Martin Van Hekken); fig. 2.21 (Library of Congress, Prints and Photographs Division, National Photo Company Collection); figs. 6.8, 10.5 (Anne Pelicano); fig. 7.1 (courtesy Naomi Manders); fig. 5.9 (Library of Congress, Prints and Photographs Division, Detroit Publishing Company Collection); fig. 7.8 (Library of Congress, Prints and Photographs Division, LC-DIG-ggbain00396); fig. 7.9 (The War Department Field Manual FM 2-5, Cavalry Drill Regulations, Horse [March 13, 1944]); fig. 7.10 (Library of Congress, Prints and Photographs Division, photograph by Harris & Ewing, LC-DIG-hec-03285); photo on p. 170 (Jeff Adcock)

Illustrations by: Zynesia Campbell (figs. 2.8 A–E, 3.1, 3.2, 3.13, 3.14, 3.15 A, 3.16 A & B, 3.19 A & B, 3.21, 7.12, 7.13 A & B, 7.14); Rick Pelicano (figs. 3.23, 8.1–8.13, 11.1, 11.2); Anne Pelicano (fig. 7.15 A–C); Steven Hutchinson (fig. 7.15 D)

Cartoon art by Gary Jones

INDEX

One day during a detail, several fellow police officers decided to play a joke on me. While on a break they unloaded my horse, Guy, from the trailer and then re-loaded him—backward! So apparently, he's happy to go on a horse trailer, whichever way he might be facing.